SURPLUS LABOUR AND THE CITY
A Study of Bombay

SURPLUS LABOUR AND THE CITY
A Study of Bombay

HEATHER JOSHI
and
VIJAY JOSHI

DELHI
OXFORD UNIVERSITY PRESS
BOMBAY CALCUTTA MADRAS
1976

Oxford University Press

OXFORD LONDON GLASGOW NEW YORK
TORONTO MELBOURNE WELLINGTON CAPE TOWN
IBADAN NAIROBI DAR ES SALAAM LUSAKA ADDIS ABABA
KUALA LUMPUR SINGAPORE JAKARTA HONG KONG TOKYO
DELHI BOMBAY CALCUTTA MADRAS KARACHI

Printed in India
by Delhi Press, New Delhi 110055
and published by C. H. Lewis, Oxford University Press
2/11 Ansari Road, Daryaganj, New Delhi 110002

PREFACE

This work is intended as a contribution to the study of urban employment problems in developing countries. It seemed worthwhile to focus attention on a single city while keeping the broader economic context firmly in view. The result is, at the very least, a detailed study of some aspects of the economy of Bombay. This is contained in Chapters II-V which examine employment, income distribution and migration patterns in the city and the interrelationships between them. Chapters I and VI are more analytical, concerned with conceptual and policy questions of wider relevance. We hope that the work, taken as a whole, throws some light on the nature of the employment problem in India (and other labour-surplus developing countries) and on policies to combat it—issues which have been and will continue to be of importance for some time to come.

Work on this book was financed by grants from the Nuffield College (Oxford) Project (supported by the Leverhulme Foundation), Merton College (Oxford) and the Institute of Economic Growth (Delhi). We are grateful to them all. Much of the gathering of data was carried out during the authors'· tenure as Visiting Fellows of the Institute of Economic Growth (Delhi) during 1971.

The completion of the work was facilitated by secretarial and research assistance and also the intellectual stimulation provided by the various academic institutions with which we have been associated: Merton College (Oxford), Institute of Economics and Statistics (Oxford), Institute of Commonwealth Studies (Oxford) and the Institute of Economic Growth (Delhi).

Of the many individuals who have helped us some must be specifically mentioned. Economic research in India is difficult without the help of someone who can provide access to the right people and sources of information. R. C. Joshi, I.C.S., formerly Commissioner of Bombay Division, fulfilled this role admirably. Without his patient guidance this work could not have been completed. Of the

others in Bombay who gave us valuable help we would like to
mention, in particular, T. R. Bhagwat, L. C. Joshi, V. V. Karjatkar
and M. A. Telang. We have benefited greatly from conversations
with academic colleagues, in particular, S. Anand, P. Collier, A.
Dasgupta, M. Datta-Chaudhuri, C. K. Hanumantha Rao, P. C.
Joshi, A. M. Khusro, R. Mabro, A. K. Sen, F. Stewart, P. P.
Streeten and P. M. Visaria. We received useful comments on parts
of the draft from E. Eshag, C. Hardy, A. Hone, I. M. D. Little, R.
Sabot and M. FG. Scott.

September 1974   H.J. & V.J.
Oxford

CONTENTS

TABLES

SURPLUS LABOUR AND THE CITY

CHAPTER ONE

SURPLUS LABOUR AND THE EMPLOYMENT PROBLEM

In India, as in many developing countries, the 'employment problem' is a subject of concern and controversy. It has become apparent that the growth of the labour force is so rapid in relation to the capacity of the economy to ensure earning opportunities that millions will be condemned to poverty for a long time to come— unless there are drastic changes in the direction of economic development. This study is concerned with the urban dimension of this problem, the empirical work being centred round a single city, Bombay. But as we shall see when discussing policy matters, no sensible judgement is possible without taking an integrated view of the wider economy.

To begin with, it is essential to be clear about the nature of the so-called 'employment problem', a popular term which can be very misleading if it is not carefully interpreted. Governments may take a narrow view of what constitutes a problem, and therefore of how to solve it, but this should not limit the social scientist's field of inquiry. In practice, government concern and action are most likely to be precipitated if there are vocal and powerful groups demanding attention, and especially if there are threats to law and order. In this study we treat as a problem any situation where social objectives are inadequately met because of obstacles which are amenable to change, irrespective of whether the actors in such a situation regard it as constituting a problem for themselves or behave in such a way as to constitute a threat to other people. Social objectives are not easy to specify. For simplicity, we assume that economic policy has as its fundamental objective the improvement of living standards generally and especially those of the poor. Among the many constraints, a critical and relevant one is the growth of the labour force which, over the next two decades at least, is almost totally beyond control. Even if population growth could be reduced, the new entrants into the labour force over this time-period have already been born.[1] The 'employment problem' refers to the imbalance between the size and growth of the labour force on the one hand, and the opportunities for economic activity offered by the existing economic structure on the other.

This is a useful statement to make even though the concepts of 'labour force' and 'economic activity' are both quite treacherous. *Economic activity* is logically prior. It is a concept whose boundaries are difficult to determine, especially where they do not coincide with the sphere of life which is channelled through market institutions. For practical purposes arbitrary lines have to be drawn. Compilers of official statistics, such as censuses and national accounts, exclude from the economic sphere certain activities like housework or raising funds for charities, and in this study we shall, on the whole, follow these conventions. The *labour force* consists of all those who are able and willing to engage in economic activity, whether or not they are actually performing it. Numbering the labour force poses both conceptual and statistical problems. The very young and the very old will almost invariably be outside the labour force. But in the case of many other groups, whether or not they are willing (and expected) to engage in economic activity will depend on cultural factors, on the returns expected from working and on the probability of their finding economic work. Given the arbitrary definition of economic activity, as well as the possibility of individuals dividing some arbitrarily defined 'working day' between 'economic' and 'non-economic' activities, the identification of members of the labour force becomes conceptually arbitrary and difficult in practice. For example, the classification of women in peasant societies as 'unpaid family labour' or as 'non-workers' can present a problem to which there is no satisfactory solution (and seems to have been settled in such dramatically different ways by the Indian Censuses of 1961 and 1971 that the absolute number of workers in the country appeared to have fallen during a period when the population increased by over 100 million). In spite of these difficulties, there is an obvious truth in the common-sense statement that the bad matching between demographic and economic structures creates a severe problem.

While we follow current usage in calling this an 'employment problem', this is not, in our view, a particularly happy choice of words. It tends to suggest that employment is an objective in its own right, that the extent of the problem is to be measured by the volume of unemployment and that the creation of more jobs is sufficient to solve it. Employment is, very largely, a means to an end rather than an end in itself. Its importance rests mainly on the contribution it makes to producing output and to creating incomes. From the *production* point of view, unemployment is a waste, a loss of potential output which could be used for any purpose society deems desirable. From the *income* point of view, unemployment deprives those affected by it of the means of earning a living. Very few people, in practice, have unearned incomes and it is a difficult undertaking, especially in poor societies, to maintain the unemployed by social security programmes. We argue, however, that while it is important for both these reasons that people should find work opportunities, the adverse effects on production and incomes arise as much from the unsatisfactory *quality* of employment as from its inadequate *quantity*. As significant as the increasing unemployment in India is the highly distorted way in which the existing economic structure absorbs large quantities of labour. It follows that while provision of more jobs is one prong of the required strategy, improving the earning ability of some of those already at work is equally necessary, involving wide-ranging policies to create, re-allocate and redistribute resources. We would not wish to deny, of course, that employment has social and psychological consequences which are important in their own right. It is clearly true that in certain cultural milieux, unemployment leads to frustration and loss of self-respect which could culminate in disorder and violence. We ourselves believe that this *expectations* dimension of employment is not of prime importance for economic policy in India. It certainly affects the educated unemployed, but, as we have argued, the urgency and acuteness of the various forms of the employment problem is not to be measured by the ability of the various victims to draw attention to themselves. Here we need only point out that even if this expectations aspect is considered to be important, its fulfilment is as much a matter of job-satisfaction arising from the quality and suitability of the jobs available as it is of their quantity *per se*. In sum, if one insists on using the term 'employment problem' to denote the consequences of the excessive growth of the labour force, one must recognize that it encompasses much more than the volume of unemployment.[2]

In the developed countries, it has for some time been the con-
vention to define unemployment as being involuntarily out of work
and to measure it as the number of people on the register of the
employment exchanges. Such a concept of unemployment would
be utterly misleading in the measurement of the 'employment
problem' in a country like India.[3] Obviously, the coverage of employment exchanges is much too limited, but that is not the basic
difficulty. The limitation applies equally to censuses and sample
surveys which use the criterion of 'not working and available for,
or seeking, work'. 'Not working' is taken to mean not having worked
on a single day during the reference period, which is generally a
week or a fortnight preceding enumeration. This part of the criterion would isolate all non-workers. The second part distinguishes
idle members of the labour force among them. It is applied rather
more stringently in urban areas where the respondent needs to have
been in search of a job to count as unemployed; in rural areas it is
sufficient for him to claim that he is 'available for work'. There are
two reasons why these criteria are irrelevant. The first point is that
the absence of a social security system in India means that complete
idleness would be avoided as far as possible by most people. In a
country like the U.K., workers can *afford* to be idle while they look
for suitable jobs. In India, doles do not exist, and the willingness
of families to support totally idle members (especially males of
working age) is limited by sheer poverty. A vast majority of people
must, therefore, do some work, however unproductive or ill paid,
simply in order to survive. The second point is that in an economy
in which a significant proportion of the labour force consists of
the self-employed and of unpaid family workers, people are much
less likely than in wage-based economies to be openly and visibly
looking for jobs on the labour market. In periods of slack activity,
the self-employed are quite likely simply to accept cuts in their
incomes and unpaid family workers to drop out of the labour force
altogether. They may well be 'available' for more work in their own
family enterprises but not outside, a distinction too subtle for
most surveys to detect. It is not very surprising, then, to find that
attempts by censuses and sample surveys to measure involuntary
unemployment in India have turned up very low rates, seldom
above 4 per cent of the labour force.

The pressure of labour supply in India is manifested not in open
unemployment but in other ways. It may lead to partial idleness,

voluntary or involuntary. In many cases, it may not be reflected in idleness at all but simply in the low productivity of work. Each of these phenomena deserves further consideration. Involuntary under-employment undoubtedly exists in the sense that there are people who would like to work longer hours at existing rates of remuneration but cannot find the work. Labour markets do not clear in such a way as to balance exactly the supply and demand for labour. Even in as labour-intensive an activity as construction, for example, there is some economic limit to how much labour can profitably be employed. Beyond a point, the loss of output involved in workers getting in each other's way may make it un-economic to expand employment however low wages may be. There could also be other reasons why employers are deterred from bidding wages down beyond a point. Even in a nominally free labour market, employers may not want to offer wages below what is generally regarded as an unacceptably low level. This need not necessarily be due to the employer succumbing to his own altruism or that of others. Starvation wages may reduce workers' productivity so sharply as to result in lower profits and costs of management may increase with the size of the labour force. All these points apply in agricultural activities as well, where there is, in addition, an important seasonal element. During the slack season, there is an acute shortage of work for landless labourers. To measure the extent of involuntary under-employment requires a survey of hours worked and of the availability of people for extra work. There has not been much research on this but what there has been appears to show that about 10 per cent of the labour force satisfies the double criterion of 'being severely under-employed' (i. e. working less than 28 hours a week) *and* of being 'available for additional work'.[4] Some doubt may be cast on these figures since there is no specific question about the wage rates at which they would be so available. But it seems a reasonable presumption that most res-pondents assumed that existing wage rates in the area are implied in the questions about availability for extra work.

In addition to those who are involuntarily under-employed, there are undoubtedly many who are 'content' to work short hours or at very low intensity in relation to what might generally be con-sidered to be the norm in this respect. Personal, social, and cultural factors may account for some of the variation in the work people intend to perform, but within a given population much of this

voluntary under-employment could be a perfectly rational response
to the low returns from working harder. On a family farm of a
very small size, to take an example, the marginal return to the
additional man-hour may be so low that there is no incentive to
work beyond a point and work-sharing between family members
may leave each one of them with time to spare. A poor, under-
nourished, landless labourer, to give another example, may refuse
to take on extra arduous work on a rural works project if it is
very badly paid. In fact, this may be one reason among many
why public works programmes in some parts of India have re-
portedly been faced with labour shortages.[5] It should not be un-
questioningly assumed that voluntary under-employment can be
excluded from the scope of the 'employment problem'. The extent
of voluntary idleness depends on particular configurations of rates
of remuneration and distributions of resources. As we shall see
below, wage rates in the organized sector of the economy are substantially higher than the supply price of labour. The share of this
sector in the available capital resources may also be excessive.
Thus, in relation to a situation in which labour and capital are
more efficiently deployed—arguably a more appropriate reference
point than the existing situation—many of the so-called voluntarily
under-employed outside the modern sector could well be available
for extra work.

A very important manifestation of the 'employment problem' is
the phenomenon of the 'working poor' who may perform a great
deal of work of very low productivity. 'Working a great deal' may
mean spending a large number of hours on the job, or working
very hard in the physical sense or both. An example of the former
would be self-employed workers such as shopkeepers, taxi-drivers
or shoe-shine boys who spend long hours soliciting custom or
waiting for customers even though they do not necessarily spend
much time actually performing the services they purvey. This might
be either because of an excessive number of sellers in the market
(who are in effect sharing work) or because the nature of demand
is for someone always to be in attendance because the call for the
tasks they perform is sporadic and unpredictable. (This also applies,
for example, to domestic servants.[6]) However, many of the working
poor do not work at low intensity. Some of the hardest physical
labour is performed by people who earn very little for doing so—
for example anyone providing transport by human traction, such

as rickshaw pullers or headload carriers. Wherever the return to work is low, as a result of the lack of resources, primitiveness of technology or low wages, people may find it necessary to work very hard and very long hours simply to keep body and soul together. Now, on conventional definitions the 'working poor' would certainly not be included in the 'employment problem' but we think there is good reason for doing so, because their poverty and low productivity are not just the result of inefficiency on their part or of the general shortage of other productive resources but in some measure of the lopsided deployment of these resources. This, in our view, is the neglected dimension of the pressure of labour supply; one which is not easily evoked by the phrase 'employment problem'.[7]

We have been leading up to a distinction which is basic and essential for an understanding of the Indian economy. This is the difference between the modern economy with its organized and protected labour market and its extensive privileges, and the rest of the economy—the traditional, self-employment and small-scale sectors. The organized sector is to be found mainly (though not exclusively) in urban areas and covers modern manufacturing industry, government and the services feeding them. In this sector, labour productivity is high, incomes even of the unskilled are relatively high, and conditions of work and service are safeguarded by labour legislation. Those who participate in this part of the economy share to some extent in the fruits of economic modernization, but the numbers doing so are limited by the capital intensity of the technology involved and the high cost of labour to employers, themselves partly the result of government policy and the self-interest of the favoured groups. The rest of the labour force must either be totally unemployed (and that is not possible for many for any length of time) or be engaged in some economic activity outside the organized sector. This unorganized sector clearly covers most rural activities but also, as we emphasize in this study, a substantial part of the urban economy. Those who fail to secure employment in the modern, organized sector are forced into the unorganized sector which has the capacity to absorb them either as casual labour, low wage employees in small enterprises, as self-employed or family workers. But this sector does not have the capacity to provide them with stable, regular, protected jobs or satisfactory incomes. No doubt, the organized sector too harbours a labour surplus in the

form of evident overmanning in the offices and factories, epito-
mized by idle peons and unnecessary industrial helpers. But the
employment problem in the sense of inadequate work and low
productivity is concentrated *par excellence* in the unorganized
sector.[8]

To recapitulate, the rapid growth of the labour force in India
creates a syndrome which we term, rather misleadingly, the 'employment problem'. It is not a synonym for un- or under-employment.
No doubt, there are many idle people who are also willing to work.
No doubt, to take an aspect of unemployment which has been
emphasized by some writers, there are activities which harbour
'surplus labour' in the sense that some workers could be removed
without affecting output. The problem, however, is wider in that
the dualism of the economy also leads to large numbers of workers
being absorbed in marginal jobs of very low productivity outside
the organized sector. Although the latter shows high labour productivity, its techniques and technology are not geared to utilizing
abundant labour. While the 'employment problem' is thus wider
than that of under-employment, it is not, however, so wide a term
as to mean just poverty or underdevelopment. Poverty is partly
a matter of the overall shortage of capital and skills in relation to
labour in India and even if perfect policies were pursued, poverty
could not be eliminated for a long time. It would be starry-eyed to
believe anything else. However, there is more to the Indian problem than simply the poverty that follows from a general shortage
of resources. The additional element is the unsuitable economic
structure which leads to output being below what it could be and
poverty being worse than it need be, even after making allowance
for resource scarcities. The 'employment problem', then, is a port-
manteau term embracing the various effects of the pressure of
numbers upon a distorted and dualistic economic structure.

We now turn briefly to policies for combating the employment
problem and the issues they raise, postponing an extended discussion to the last chapter. Relevant policies would help the under-
employed by increasing the availability of work and both the under-
employed and the 'working poor' by increasing the productivity
of their activities. The first category would include measures to
increase labour absorption and utilization in the relatively capital-
intensive parts of industry and agriculture or at least to prevent
further increases in their capital intensity. It would also include

special employment-creation programmes such as rural public works. The second category would consist of measures to improve the productivity of activities which are already sufficiently labour-intensive by channelling capital, education and technical assistance in their direction. All these policies would have to operate on a broad front through the price mechanism, through the government budget and through direct intervention. Formulating the details of these policies would be a task of some complexity for two reasons:

(a) There is the difficulty that indiscriminate expansion of employment and/or encouragement of the unorganized sector might reduce the level or growth of output. There would be adverse effects on the level of output if the activities to which resources are directed are technologically 'inferior' and on the growth of output if such a diversion leads to reduced saving and investment. Such possibilities must clearly be considered (though there has been little hard evidence for the operation of such effects). It may be possible to avoid them by exercising sufficient care in the selection of activities for promotion. A further point is that when a genuine trade-off does exist between higher incomes for the poor and higher levels or growth of output, it need not necessarily be resolved in favour of the latter. If the favourable effect on output is not expected to 'trickle down' to the poor, or to be redistributed to them by the government, it may be quite rational to forgo output for the sake of the welfare of the poorer groups.

(b) There is the difficulty that the proposed strategy may not be politically feasible. It might be argued that increases in the living standards of the poor must involve some sacrifices by the upper income groups who are bound to resist them. We think that this is too hopeless a view. Redistribution of *existing* assets and extra taxation of existing incomes may be difficult but there would be less resistance to diverting *new* investment in the way we suggest. Part of new asset-creation and increases in national income would accrue to the poorer groups but this is quite different from taxing or confiscating incomes and assets which already belong to the upper income groups. 'Redistribution by stealth' may thus be a practical possibility, especially if supplemented by a campaign to convince vested interests that the explosive consequences of present trends would be much worse than those of acquiescence in the programme.

The empirical part of our study concentrates on employment in

Bombay in the nineteen-sixties. The employment problem in urban areas has not received much theoretical or empirical analysis. It involves in addition to the aspects mentioned before, many other complications. One must consider the complex but fascinating question of rural-urban migration and its relevance for development policies. Nor can one devise such policies without considering the economies of urban agglomeration on the one hand and the overhead costs of urbanization on the other. We have chosen to look at only one city because, although a certain amount of data on employment in all urban areas of India is available, it covers such a wide range of conditions in towns and cities of different regions, sizes and economic functions that information on developments for this heterogeneous aggregate are extremely difficult to interpret. Furthermore, as will become apparent, comparison of data from different sources requires great care and attention to detail which would not be feasible when using geographically aggregated data. The study of Bombay in particular may have some wider relevance since, as one of the largest, most industrialized and Westernized metropolitan centres in India, developments there may hold lessons about the shape of things to come, or to be avoided, elsewhere.

After a brief introduction to the city in its historical and geographical setting, we attempt to describe and compare the demographic and economic structures of the city. The latter involves a detailed description of the different types of work being performed by the economically active population at the beginning of the sixties, and the wide range of incomes that could be earned in the city. The dynamics of the situation are introduced in an analysis of changes in the structure of employment during the decade 1961-71 and a discussion of the role of migration in the city's labour supply. Throughout, we emphasize the distinction between the organized and unorganized sectors. In the final chapter we discuss the implications of the evidence presented for economic policy in the country as a whole and in Bombay in particular. Part of the object of this last chapter is to clarify the various choices which have to be faced and to indicate the judgements of fact and value that are required in making these choices. Our empirical work throws some light on the subject but a great deal of research still remains to be done.

We ought to make a disclaimer at this stage. This analysis is by no means a complete socio-economic study of life and labour in Bombay. We do not say enough about industrial relations and trade unions; the quality and skills of the labour force; the potential flexibility of techniques in the organized sector nor about technical conditions of production in either sector, though these are all topics of importance for employment policy. The reader will doubtless raise other questions whose existence we have not even acknowledged. The scope of the empirical study was restricted by our reliance on secondary, though not necessarily published, sources. Many questions arose which could only be answered by collection of information first-hand. Our resulting concentration on the distinction between two sections of the working population gives a one-dimensional sketch of a multi-dimensional subject, a sketch which unfortunately, and perhaps obtrusively, lacks much detail and colour. We believe, however, that in focussing on the difference between the organized and unorganized sectors, we have isolated a phenomenon of crucial relevance for Indian economic development.

NOTES

1   The labour force in India, which, using the definitions of the 1961 Census, was about 200 million at the beginning of the 1970s, is expected to increase by more than 70 million during the decade. About 50 million of these people will have to earn their livelihood in rural areas and the rest in urban areas. (See Appendix V of the *Report of the Committee of Experts on Unemployment Estimates*, Planning Commission, Government of India, 1970). It is implicit in these remarks that there is only limited scope for adjustment of labour supply to demand through changes in the proportion of the adult population participating in the labour force. This is plausible enough, as such an adjustment is more likely to involve female participation rates than those of males, but these are already fairly low, and, at least in urban areas, subject to opposite, upward pressures from other social and economic forces.

2   For the distinction between the production, income and expectations aspects of employment, see A.K. Sen, *Employment, Technology and Development* (Oxford University Press, Oxford and New York, 1975). Though we have used his terminology, his distinctions are not quite the same as ours. In particular, he identifies the production aspect of the 'employment problem' with 'surplus labour' in the strict sense

meaning the existence of a situation in which withdrawal of workers from some activities would leave output unchanged. We have adopted a wider standpoint. Useful analytical discussions of the employment problem (with which we do not necessarily agree) are also to be found in the *Report of the Committee of Experts on Unemployment Estimates* (Planning Commission, Government of India, 1970), in David Turnham, *The Employment Problem in Developing Countries* (O.E.C.D., Paris, 1970), in the I.L.O. Report on Kenya, *Employment, Incomes and Equality* (Geneva, 1972), and in Raj Krishna, 'Unemployment in India' *Economic and Political Weekly*, March 1973.

3   There are difficulties in measuring involuntary unemployment in developed countries as well, arising from the dependence of the propensity to register on the confidence placed by the unemployed on their chances of finding a job. Further, even if open unemployment can be measured, it is only an index of the under-utilization of labour, not of its misallocation. Nicholas Kaldor, for example, has suggested that the U.K. suffers from a 'labour surplus' in the service sector coupled with a 'labour constraint' in the manufacturing sector which leads to a reduction in the growth of output below its potential.

4   See Raj Krishna, op. cit.

5   For further evidence, see M. L. Dantwala, 'Approaches to Growth and Employment', *Economic and Political Weekly*, December 1972.

6   If we take a view about *normal* work-intensity this category of people could be assimilated with the under-employed discussed earlier.

7   We have distinguished between the 'employment problem' and involuntary un- and under-employment, the latter consisting of those who are idle *and* willing to work more. Some writers emphasize that under-employment has a production aspect. From the production point of view, a man is under-employed if he can be removed from his present occupation without output being affected. Even if we postulate individuals rationally choosing between leisure and income, the above situation does not imply a zero marginal product of labour and hence zero marginal valuation of leisure. In a definitive paper, A. K. Sen has shown that strict surplus labour of this kind is compatible with a positive marginal product of labour and requires only that the marginal valuation of leisure be *constant* over the relevant range (see A. K. Sen, 'Peasants and Dualism, With and Without Surplus Labour', *Journal of Political Economy*, 1966). If such is the case, the withdrawal of a man and his labour is compensated by those left behind working harder to keep output constant. In *Employment, Technology and Development*, op. cit., Sen makes the valuable point that under-employment estimates could be based on different concepts and that they are appropriate for different purposes. The estimate of involuntary under-employment could differ from the estimate of under-employment as meaning strict surplus labour, if the 'strictly surplus labourers' did not declare themselves to be available for extra work. If individuals' optima are characterized by a constant marginal valuation of leisure, it is not clear whether they would want extra work or not. Though Sen does not bring

this out, under this assumption the distinction between voluntary and involuntary under-employment becomes fuzzy. On these matters see also Raj Krishna (op. cit.).

In an interesting paper (S. Mehra, 'Surplus Labour in Indian Agriculture', *Indian Economic Review*, 1966), Sakuntala Mehra has calculated that 17 per cent of the Indian agricultural labour force is strictly surplus. Her method consists of classifying farms by time worked per cultivator and assuming that all farms with less than the highest time worked per cultivator are functioning on a strictly surplus labour basis. This assumption which amounts to saying that the marginal valuation of leisure is constant, may reasonably be questioned.

In our view, it would be unnecessarily restrictive to define the 'employment problem' to mean the existence of strict surplus labour. There are people who are not surplus in the strict sense, but whose productivity is very low. They may be voluntarily under-employed or they may be working very hard indeed. To exclude such people from the scope of the 'employment problem' would be to ignore a salient aspect of the pressure of numbers.

8 Other terms used in the literature (for example in writings associated with the I.L.O's World Employment Programme) are 'protected' and 'unprotected' sectors or 'formal' and 'informal' sectors.

CHAPTER TWO

BOMBAY : POPULATION AND LABOUR FORCE

A. THE CITY

Bombay is located on the Western coast of India on what is now a peninsula, with the business centre of the city at its southern tip. This peninsula was once a group of islands which are now joined to each other and the mainland by land reclamation that has been going on for several centuries. Between the one-time islands and the mainland lies a stretch of water which forms an excellent natural harbour and which attracted the original settlement of the place by European traders. Bombay Island was ceded by the Portuguese to the British in 1665. Since then the city has grown to be one of the largest in the world, the second largest in India after Calcutta. In 1971 the population of the municipality (which includes the suburban extensions into the north of the peninsula) was nearly six million, and satellite towns and industries had also been growing up very rapidly on the adjoining mainland. The city accounted for over one per cent of India's entire population, and nearly six per cent of its urban population.

It is the largest industrial centre of Maharashtra, one of the most industrialized states of the Indian Union. It has been a leading centre of the cotton-mill industry for over a century, and more recently engineering and chemical industries have grown up. Besides manufacturing, the city retains the functions which brought it into existence as an administrative, communications and trading centre serving Western India: it has also become the leading business and commercial centre of India, housing the headquarters of many public and private sector corporations. In many ways, not only as the point of landing of the King Emperor in 1911, Bombay has been the 'Gateway of India' for the West. Here, Western influence has been felt most intensively and effectively. The Bombay area has experienced much of the modernization on the Western model which as yet has not penetrated so deeply in other parts of

the country. Nevertheless, along with this prosperity there is ample
evidence of Asian poverty. As new multi-storey blocks appear, so
too do squalid colonies of hutment dwellings. Both the rich and
the poor have crowded into the city.

The sense of overcrowding is enhanced by the geographical situation, once so suitable for a fortified anchorage but now severely
restricting expansion in all but one direction—further on to the
mainland and further away from the focal point of the city, which
is much more graphically described as 'downtown' rather than
'centre'. Hundreds of thousands of commuters travel to work each
day along the choked arteries of the one-ended linear city. The
development of the downtown area for offices, hotels and luxury
apartments continues, with high-rise building and land reclamation,
involving the usual private profits and social costs—the latter
through the overloading of the utility and transit networks, developments in which struggle to keep pace. There is also extension
of activity, such as the dispersal of manufacturing investment, to the
mainland. It is hoped that the construction of a new port and the
establishment of the Twin City across the bay will act as a counter-
focus to ease the congestion in the mother city.

However, the emphasis in this Metropolitan Plan on the modern
economy of the Five Year Plans and on the problems of urban
congestion may treat the place too much like part of an advanced
country. It is in a very poor country and a large part of its own
population live at very low levels and work outside the modern
economy. Urban congestion may not be the most pressing of their
problems and may also not be a problem that planners can consis-
tently study in isolation. It is not unlikely that, if improvements
touched the living conditions of the poor in Bombay and not elsewhere, their present situation would soon be re-occupied by people
coming in from outside. Our study concentrates upon this aspect of
Indian urbanization.

B. DEMOGRAPHY

Migrants and the Demographic Structure in 1961

The latest detailed demographic information available is from the
Census of 1961. At the time of writing only very broad totals were
available for 1971. Table II. 1 shows these totals and the structure
of the population in 1961 by age, sex and place of birth.

Table II.1

The Demographic Structure of Population in Bombay, 1961, and Population Totals, 1971

Thousands

Age	Total Population			Migrants		Non-migrants	
	Persons	Males	Females	Males	Females	Males	Females
1971							
All ages	5,971	3,478	2,492	n.a.	n.a.	n.a.	n.a.
1961							
All ages	4,152	2,496	1,657	1,699	939	798	717
0-4	459	235	224	49	47	185	177
5-9	463	237	226	72	69	166	157
10-14	390	211	179	89	71	121	109
15-19	365	218	147	151	85	67	62
20-24	516	324	192	254	133	70	58
25-29	499	317	182	269	140	47	42
30-34	398	262	136	228	107	33	29
35-39	309	210	99	182	78	28	20
40-44	234	160	74	138	58	21	16
45-49	166	110	56	93	43	17	12
50-54	136	88	49	74	38	14	11
55-59	77	49	28	41	22	8	6
60+	141	77	65	58	48	18	17

SOURCES : 1971. *Census of India 1971*, Series II—Maharashtra, pt. II-A, General Population Tables.

1961. K. C. Zachariah, *Migrants in Greater Bombay* (Bombay 1968), Table 5.1, based upon *Census of India 1961*, vol. X, pt. (1-B), Greater Bombay Census Tables, Table C-IV, and vol. X, pt. X (1-C), Special Migration Table II.

NOTE: In the *Census of India*, 'Migrant' in general refers to a person born outside the place of enumeration. In this table, and all following tables (unless otherwise specified), the term 'Migrant' refers to persons born outside Greater Bombay but within the Indian sub-continent. Persons born in foreign countries other than Pakistan are included among Non-Migrants because no detailed information about them was included in the Special Migration Tables of the Census.

As is the case with most cities, especially those which are growing rapidly, Bombay had acquired much of its population through in-migration rather than natural reproduction *in situ*. A large proportion of its inhabitants (in 1961, 64 per cent of persons, 69

per cent of males and 57 per cent of females) had been born outside
the city.[1] This gave it a distinctive demographic structure. Males
substantially outnumbered females, and the age structure, particularly of the male population, was heavily weighted in favour of
working age-groups. It does not show the normal pyramid shape
as some adult age-groups outnumber younger age-groups. 70 per
cent of Bombay's male population was aged between 15 and 59,
whereas for India as a whole the proportion was 54 per cent. The
age and sex composition of the population born in Bombay is
more or less normal, but that of the non-native, or migrant population is very distorted. The excess of males is far more marked
among migrants[2] and it is the age-structure of the population born
outside the city which imposes its diamond shape on the age pyramid. Migration is typically of people—largely men—who spend
their childhood in their places of birth, come to Bombay during
their adult lives, and who may also leave the city in their old age or
even sooner.

Many of the migrants are young single men who have come to the
city in early adulthood before marrying, but more than half of the
excess of adult males over adult females (787,000) was accounted
for by an excess of currently married males over currently married
females, of 454,000. This indicates that many of the married migrants' wives (and hence children) remain outside the city during
at least some of the husband's sojourn in town. Not all of the men
without women live on their own in the city. Many are accom-
modated in extended family households by their kinsmen and others
band together to form all-male households known as 'chummeries'.
Evidence on the size and composition of households is discussed
in Appendix II.1.

The inhabitants of Bombay had come there from all parts of
India as well as further afield, and between them had as many as
214 different mother tongues. As is shown in Table II. 2, a majority
had been born in Western India, but the city's catchment area
spreads beyond—to the south and north of the sub-continent.
Fewer come from the north-east. Most of those born in Pakistan
were refugees from the time of Partition. This table shows persons
of various origins as a proportion of the city's population and, to
give an idea of the extent to which various parts of the country are
'represented', migrants as a proportion of the population at origin.
This standardization procedure (col. 4) shows that the large Hindi-

Table II.2

The Population of Bombay and their Places of Birth, 1961

Place of Origin	Persons in Bombay by Birthplace		Population at Origin	Migrants per 1000 Population at Origin:	
	'000	per 1000 in city	'000	in Bombay	in urban India
	(1)	(2)	(3)	(4)	(5)
WESTERN INDIA					
Greater Bombay	1485	356			
Elsewhere in					
Maharashtra specifically :	1111	266	35402	31	108
Ratnagiri	*494*	*119*	*1827*	*270*	
Satara	*141*	*34*	*1430*	*98*	
Poona	*118*	*28*	*2467*	*47*	
Kolaba	*109*	*26*	*1059*	*104*	
Thana	*45*	*11*	*1653*	*27*	
21 other districts	*203*	*49*	*26966*	*8*	
Gujarat[a]	451	108	20691	22	112
Goa	83	20	627	132	320
SOUTH INDIA					
Mysore	172	41	23587	7	84
Kerala[b]	74	18	16928	4	62
Andhra Pradesh	90	22	35983	3	78
Madras & Pondicherry	85	21	34056	3	94
NORTH & CENTRAL INDIA					
U.P. & Bihar	326	78	120202	3	55
Rajasthan, Punjab, etc.[c]	95	23	48033	2	79
Madhya Pradesh	23	6	32372	1	51
EASTERN INDIA[d]	16	4	66904	—	37
ALL INDIA			439235	6	70
Pakistan	111	27			
Other Countries	29	7			
Unknown	1	—			
TOTAL	4152	1000			

NOTES : (a) Includes Dadra & Nagar Haveli.

(b) Includes Laccadive, Minicoy & Amindivi Islands.

(c) Includes Delhi, Himachal Pradesh, Jammu & Kashmir.

(d) West Bengal, Assam, Orissa, Manipur, Tripura, N.E.F.A., Nagaland, Sikkim, Andaman & Nicobar Islands.

(e) This applies to the whole state. The denominator includes the population of Bombay since it was impossible not to include out-migrants from the city in the numerator.

SOURCES: *Census of India 1961*, vol. I, pt. II-C, Table D-II; vol. X, pt. II-A and pt. X (1-B), Table D-II.

speaking contingent from U.P. and Bihar is smaller in relation to
the size of the population at home than the migrants from somewhat smaller places which are on the whole nearer Bombay—the
states of South India, and more especially Goa. The ratios shown
in column 4 can be taken as an indicator of the propensity to migrate towards Bombay from these areas.[3] Column 5 is included
for comparison and shows the ratio of migrants enumerated in all
urban destinations in India to the population at origin. Although
those regions with a low representation in Bombay have sent emi-
grants to other urban areas, areas within the orbit of Bombay
seem on the whole to be among those with high propensities to
send migrants to urban areas.

However, the broad regional figures hide some very great variations in migration from different places. As can be seen from the
table, five out of the twenty-six districts in Maharashtra accounted
for over eighty per cent of all the migrants from the state; other
districts are scarcely more heavily represented in Bombay than the
populations from several other states. Although the specified districts are in Western Maharashtra, it is not proximity to Bombay
alone which accounts for their over-representation. The district
with the biggest single contingent in Bombay is not immediately
adjacent to the city, as are Thana and Kolaba; it is Ratnagiri,
which lies along the coast to the south and has traditionally, for at
least a century, been sending the sons of its soil to Bombay and to
its cotton mills in particular. Some recent surveys[4] suggest that
further disaggregation of the data down to village level would
show considerable local variations in propensities to out-migrate,
and to migrate to Bombay in particular. Although these pieces of
evidence only apply to one part of Maharashtra, it would seem
very likely that there is much intra-state and intra-district variation
in rates of migration to Bombay in other parts of India. Such an
effect would be produced if the establishment of a habit of migration and channels of information (through contacts with previous
migrants) between particular pairs of places had led to an uneven
development of migration streams.[5]

There is also considerable variation, not shown in detail here,
between the rates of migration of males and females and of those
with rural and urban birthplaces. Broadly speaking, one-third of
the male migrants and a slightly greater proportion of the females
had been born in urban areas. This gives an over-representation of

those born in other urban areas, especially of women, since less than one-fifth of the total population of India had urban birthplaces. The high rate of migration of urban-born females could be attributed to two factors. Firstly, male migrants from rural areas have a greater opportunity to leave their womenfolk behind in the ancestral village. Secondly, bachelors already resident in Bombay who take brides from other places may be more inclined to choose someone who has been brought up in an urban area. The overall higher propensity for the urban-born to come to Bombay reflects a greater degree of movement towards urban destinations among the urban-born as a whole. Only 5 per cent of the persons with rural birthplaces were enumerated in urban areas of India in 1961, whereas 18 per cent of those born in towns were enumerated in an urban area other than their birthplace. The census cannot tell us whether step-migration occurs as there is no indication of whether or not migrants come straight to Bombay from their birthplaces or spend time in other places on the way.

Another gap in our knowledge about migration is in the extent of out-migration, both by natives and non-natives of the city. Zachariah has inferred from the distribution of migrants by age and duration of residence that there is substantial return migration by migrants, particularly by males, both shortly after arrival in the city, and at the end of their working lives. There is also thought to be out-migration from the Bombay-born population, particularly of women at the time of marriage, as happens all over India.

Table II.3 shows the migrant population by duration of residence in the city. In 1961, 7 per cent of male migrants and 9 per cent of female migrants had been in the city for less than a year. The greater share of recent migrants among females probably reflects at least two influences. One is the delay in womenfolk coming to join men who have migrated earlier, and the second is a trend towards more migration of females.[6] The numbers of people reporting less than one year's duration of residence are approximately equal to the volume of gross migration during the year previous to the census (but are subject to a large margin of error and in addition exclude those who died or out-migrated within a year of arrival). This suggests that in-migration added about 5 per cent to Bombay's population during the year preceding the 1961 Census. The figures for 1971, being based only on a sample survey, may not be so reliable. They appear to show a sharp drop in the proportion of new

Table. II. 3

The Distribution of Migrants by their Duration of Residence in Greater Bombay and their Sex Ratio, 1961 and 1971

Duration of residence in years	Per cent						Males per thousand females	
	Persons		Males		Females			
	1961	1971	1961	1971	1961	1971	1961	1971
All durations	100.0	100.0	100.0	100.0	100.0	100.0	1811	1533
Less than 1 year	7.9	2.6	7.4	2.4	8.8	3.0	1528	1212
1-4	20.4	14.6	19.9	12.6	21.1	17.6	1714	1099
5-9	17.8	18.1	17.7	18.7	17.9	17.2	1790	1371
10-14	19.6	15.9	19.3	15.2	20.1	17.0	1748	1373
15+	34.4	48.8	35.7	51.1	32.1	45.2	2019	1733

SOURCES: *Census of India 1961* and *1971*; CIDCO Survey of 1500 households.

arrivals in the migrant population and an increase in the proportion
of females among migrants of all residence durations. The implication of this and other information for an analysis of the city's
growth is discussed next.

Population Growth

The growth of the city's population since the turn of the century,
from under one million to six million in 1971, is shown in Table
II.4. The latest decade showed the biggest ever intercensal increase
in terms of absolute numbers. The proportionate increase over
1961, 44 per cent, was surpassed only once before, between 1941
and 1951, when there was a great spurt in the growth of population
and industry in the city when war and independence followed the
Depression.

Table II.4 also shows, in the third and fourth columns, the
estimates made by K.C. Zachariah of the contribution of natural
increase and net migration to the growth of the city's population
up to 1961,[7] and some rather tentative estimates of our own of the
extent to which continued migration accounted for the growth of
Bombay in the latest decade.

Column 5 of Table II.4 shows that since 1921 the share of non-
natives in the city's population has been falling, i.e. the proportion
of the settled, city-born population has been rising. Associated
with this change has been a diminution in the demographic pecu-
liarities of the city, which, as we noted above, are characteristics
of the non-native population: the excess of males over females
has been falling and the high proportion of working-age males
has been becoming less marked (columns 6 and 7). As the share of
the city-born population increased, so too did the estimated contribution of natural increase to the city's growth (columns 3 and 4).
By 1961, nearly half of the growth of the city was assigned to natural
increase whose contribution earlier in the century had been negative,[8] and we estimate that it accounted for well over one-half of
the increase between 1961 and 1971.

The derivation of these estimates is explained in an appendix to
this chapter. Their precision is not guaranteed, but the continued
increase in the proportion of natives in the city and of natural
increase in its growth is plausible. The increased proportion of
females is a piece of hard information, and is likely to have been,
as in the past, associated with an increased share of natives in the

Table II. 4

Greater Bombay : Selected Indicators of Demographic Evolution

	Population '000	Change over previous decade '000			Percentage of migrants in total population	Percentage of male population aged 15-59	Males per thousand females		
		Total growth	Natural increase	Net migration			Total population	Migrants	Non-migrants
1901	928				76.6	75.9	1534	1830	1108
1911	1149	221	-129	350	80.4	79.0	1754	2140	1172
1921	1380	232	-168	400	84.0	81.0	1782	2068	1276
1931	1398	17	-58	75	75.4	77.5	1689	1982	1373
1941	1801	404	4	400	72.6	76.8	1624	2038	1133
1951	2994	1193	243	950	72.1	74.6	1659	1972	1133
1961	4152	1158	558	600	64.2	69.6	1507	1810	1112
1971	5971	1819	1000*	819*	54.1*	n.a.	1396	1533*	n.a.

SOURCES: K.C. Zachariah, *Migrants in Greater Bombay* and *Census of India 1971:* (Series 11, pt. II-A, General Population Tables).
*Estimates derived from CIDCO Migration Survey 1971, birth registration data, and All India mortality rates, as explained in Appendix II.2.

city.[9] Furthermore, by the end of the decade the city probably had a larger proportion of women of childbearing age among its population than ever before; so without denigrating the success of the Family Planning Programme (whose greatest impact was anyway only after 1966), an uprecedented rate of addition to the native population was to have been expected. This automatically reduces the proportionate contribution of migration to the increase. However, if the results of the Survey are to be taken seriously, it also seems that the migration was slowing down for independent reasons. In the 1971 Survey only 2½ per cent of migrants were new arrivals. According to our rather shaky edifice of assumptions, the absolute volume of both in-migration and out-migration dropped during the sixties, with the final result that the flow of net migration was larger than the six lakhs of the previous decade. Although in-migration slowed down during this period, so also had out-migration, and the flow of migrants to the city had clearly not dried up.

Variations over time in the flow of migration seem very broadly to follow the city's economic fortunes. We shall see in a later chapter that employment in Bombay stagnated during the second half of the sixties. However, the connection of this with the slowing of migration flows is not simple—labour-force growth did not in any case adjust to the rate of increase of employment; and coinciding with the industrial recession, there were bad harvests, which, other things being equal, one might have expected to lead to increased migration out of rural areas. The drought of 1972 brought many villagers towards the cities of Maharashtra. The emergency rural employment projects successfully diverted this tide, at least in the short run, but this reminds us that it is not only conditions at destination which may influence migration flows. These issues and their relation to employment problems will be resumed in a later chapter.

Whatever may be the truth about rates of migration during the sixties—a matter which further tabulations of the 1971 Census may help to clear up—we can conclude that the city is now at a stage where both possible sources of population growth are substantial, and neither should be ignored as a source of continued pressure on the city's jobs and facilities.

C. THE LABOUR FORCE

The labour force is a measure of the number of economically active people—those at work ('workers') and those not at work but available for work ('unemployed'). As emphasized in the last chapter, the concept is a tricky one. It requires prior delineation of the boundaries of 'economic' activity and, in addition, a decision about the extent of the person's total activity which has to be 'economic' before he or she is counted as economically active. On both points, the 1961 Census follows Western practice. As for the first point, economic activity is defined in such a way as to exclude from the labour force full-time students, housewives, *rentiers*, beggars, prostitutes, as well as people known to earn their income from illegal activities. On the second point the 1961 Census was fairly catholic (in contrast to the 1971 Census). The 1961 figures for 'workers' include all people who engaged in *some* economic activity whether or not it was their primary activity or occupied them full-time. This approach gives a generous estimate of workers and a conservative estimate of unemployed, so the two taken together give a fairly good idea of the number of people resident in the city at the time of the census and 'available for work' in so far as this is meaningful in the Indian context.

In 1971, the Census of India adopted a different approach, enumerating as 'workers' only those whose *main* activity was economic, not as in 1961 all those who engaged in any economic activity, whether or not this was their primary occupation. The idea was to exclude from the figure for workers, people such as housewives or students who might occasionally help in some 'economic' work but whose primary roles were outside the labour force. It was hoped that information on such people for whom economic activity is a secondary occupation would appear in later tabulations of the 1971 Census. But these tabulations in fact showed this to be an idle hope and we are effectively left with the initial results which, somewhat startlingly, report the number of workers in the whole of India in 1971 to be smaller than in 1961. The rationale and results of the changes in the Census have been hotly debated elsewhere.[10] After 1971, the elusive concept of the labour force has slipped even further from the grasp of the analyst of the Indian economy. There will be no information on the openly unemployed comparable to that from 1961, and those workers who were covered in 1961 but excluded in 1971 include some of the 'under-employed' whose economic activity was marginal because they did not get enough work, as well as those whose commitment to economic activity would be limited under any circumstances.

Table II.5 shows the relevant figures for Bombay for 1961 and 1971. In the case of Bombay, it is hardly surprising, given the more conservative enumeration of the working population, that the ratio of workers to population appears to have dropped. Table II.5 also gives our estimate of the 1971 labour force using 1961 definitions. The method used to derive this estimate is explained in Appendix II.3. The estimate has no value in itself but it becomes useful when combined with data on determinants of labour supply other than the resident labour force and information on the growth of organized employment during the decade. This task is attempted later. Incidentally, Table II.5 bears out the fact that the labour force is largely male and remains so in spite of the change in the sex-ratio between 1961 and 1971. (See Table II. 5.)

We now turn to a more detailed examination of the features of labour force participation in Bombay. For this purpose, we have to rely on data from the 1961 Census because the appropriate 1971 figures are not available; in any case, even if they were available, they would not be comparable with the 1961 figures. Tables II.6 and II.7 show labour force participation rates (i.e. workers plus unemployed divided by population) which indicate the propensity of the resident population by age, sex and educational attainment to make itself available for economic activity.

The overwhelming majority of males aged between 15 and 59 were in the labour force. There were also some workers among those outside this age group who together accounted for about 3 per cent of the male labour force. Most of the males between the ages of 15 and 60 who were not in the labour force were full-time students, as suggested by the lower participation rates of those below 25. This also accounts for the lower participation rates of males over 10 with intermediate educational achievements, since any full-time students over the age of 10 would be at least literate. Apart from this factor one can say that males aged 15-59 have an almost uniformly high labour force participation rate which is not likely to vary upwards or downwards very much.

Female participation rates were however much lower, much

Table II. 5

*Population, Workforce and Labour Force,
Greater Bombay 1961 and 1971*

	Population		Labour Force	Workers	Unem-ployed
	Total	Aged 15-59			
(Thousands)					
1961					
Persons	4,152	2,699	1,767	1,687	80
Males	2,496	1,737	1,616	1,541	75
Females	1,656	962	151	146	5
1971		(Est.)	(Est.)		
Persons	5,971	—	2,371	2,198	—
Males	3,478	2,331	2,143	2,006	—
Females	2,492	—	227	192	—
Intercensal Difference (percentage)		(Est.)	(Est.)	(Reported)	
Persons	44	—	34	30	—
Males	39	34	33	30	—
Females	50	—	50	32	—

DEFINITIONS

'Worker', in 1961, covers all persons who had engaged in economic activity on at least one of the fifteen days prior to the Census. In 1971, the coverage was changed to exclude all persons whose 'main activity' was not economic. 'Unemployed' covers those seeking work but who were not engaged for a single day during the reference period.

'Labour Force' is the sum of persons working and seeking work, i.e. workers unemployed.

SOURCES: *Census of India 1961*, vol. X, pt. (I-B) Greater Bombay Census Table, Tables B-II, B-VIII and D-IV; and *Census of India* 1971, series II—Maharashtra, pt. II-A, General Population Tables, pp 220-27.

Estimated figures in the Table (marked Est.) are derived in the manner explained in Appendix II.3.

more variable for different groups of the population and much more likely to vary over time either as a result of changes in the demographic structure or changes in the demand for labour.[11] The low female participation rates are characteristic of Indian cities. Economic and social considerations combine to keep the proportion of urban females in the work-force very low. As Myrdal

Table II. 6

Labour Force Participation by Age, Greater Bombay, 1961

Age	Persons in Labour Force per 1,000 in Population	
	Males	Females
0-14	23	8
15-19	505	87
20-24	890	138
25-34	982	155
35-59	962	178
60+	536	75
All ages	647	91

SOURCE : *Census of India 1961*, pt. X(1-B); Table B-VIII, pt. A, C-III, B-II; and P.M. Visaria, 'The Level and Pattern of Work Participation in Greater Bombay' (Bombay University, mimeo., 1970).

has said: 'An economy whose capacity to absorb men of working age is strained, does not encourage the elimination of traditional forms of discrimination against economic activity by women.'[12] Female participation rates are somewhat higher in rural areas and smaller towns because there is more economic activity which takes place within the fold of household enterprise. Those women who did work in Bombay were largely confined to a few occupations which is also symptomatic of conservative attitudes about what work is suitable for women.[13]

The effect of social inhibitions on female work participation is also seen in the varying participation rates for those with different levels of education (Table II.7). Women workers are more likely to come from the most backward or the most educationally advanced groups. The dip in participation rates for educational levels between illiterate and matriculate cannot be entirely explained as it was for males by the presence of full-time students in the denominator. A plausible hypothesis is that except for very advanced families whose women are likely to be highly educated, only those households who are in dire necessity will send their

Table II. 7

Education and Labour Force Participation, Greater Bombay, 1961

rates per thousand

Educational Level	Participation in labour force by persons aged over 10		Distribution of persons aged over 10 by Educational Category	
	Males	Females	Males	Females
All levels	798	125	1000	1000
Illiterate	914	168	261	424
Literate without educational level	803	54	261	210
Primary	684	51	318	276
Secondary	807	262	119	69
Graduate (non-technical)	895	422	24	14
Graduate (technical)	894	699	17	6

SOURCE: *Census of India 1961*, pt. X (1-B), Tables B-III pt. A, B-VIII pt. A, and C-III pt. B.

women out to work and the women in such families are likely to include a higher proportion of illiterates. Women who are slightly better off in the way of educational qualifications are likely to belong to households whose male members are sufficiently well off not to be compelled to send them into the labour market.

The net effect of low female participation rates is that Bombay's labour force is overwhelmingly male. While males outnumbered females 3 to 2 in the 41 lakh population as a whole, in the 17 lakhs of the working population there were more than 10 men for every woman. Table II.7 also describes the division of the adult population into groups with different levels of formal skills. It can be seen that a quarter of the adult males and 40 per cent of the adult females were illiterate and only a tiny minority (4 per cent of males and 2 per cent of females) had graduate qualifications.

Open Unemployment

The overall rate of unemployment in 1961 was 4.6 per cent using the entire labour force as the denominator and 5.9 per cent using

the number of employees plus the number of unemployed as the
denominator, which, perhaps more appropriately, is restricted to the
wage-labour part of the economy. Both these rates are somewhat
higher than those for All Urban India, as Table II.8 indicates. The
Census also indicates that half of those recorded as seeking work
were doing so for the first time and that more than half of them
(57 per cent) were below 25 years of age. These facts are not particularly surprising and are in line with those from other countries.

There was also an interesting and somewhat puzzling contrast
with All Urban India in the labour force's unemployment rates for
persons with different levels of education.

Table II.8

*Rates of Unemployment : Bombay & All Urban India, 1961 Census,
by Education*

	Bombay	All Urban India
Unemployed as a percentage of Labour Force:		
All Educational Levels	4.6	2.9
Without Education	3.9	2.0
Primary Education	6.0	4.7
Secondary Education	5.3	5.9
Graduate	2.3	3.3
Unemployed as percentage of Employees + Unemployed:		
All Educational Levels	5.9	5.5

SOURCE: *Census of India 1961*, General Economic Tables, and Greater Bombay
Census Tables, Tables B-VIII.A, B-III.A, B-VI.A and B.

Table II.8 shows that, while in urban India as a whole the incidence of unemployment was higher among those with education
to the secondary level and above, in Bombay unemployment rates
were higher for those with less education, especially for those with
primary education. The pattern generally prevailing at the national
level of higher unemployment among the educated could be explained by the hypothesis that it is the better educated who can
better afford to wait for a job. Within the educated group the higher
national unemployment rate for matriculates than for graduates,
which we also find in Bombay, can be explained by competition from graduates for the kind of jobs that matriculates might
hope to get. However, it is not so easy to explain why people of a

lower educational standard should be over-represented among Bombay's openly unemployed. One explanation of this may be that other parts of urban India have a relatively bigger non-wage sector. If, as is likely but not demonstrable for want of the relevant cross-tabulation in the Census, there is a higher proportion of non-wage workers among the uneducated than among the more educated, then the denominator for the All-India unemployment rates of the less educated will contain a large proportion of persons for whom the question of open unemployment does not arise. However, even after excluding non-wage labour from both labour forces, Bombay appears to have a slightly bigger incidence of unemployment than the rest of urban India, so it is worth mentioning an alternative or supplementary conjecture.

One can hazard the guess that Bombay's surplus of uneducated unemployed represents a pool of job-seekers among a floating po-pulation of recently arrived migrants. There is no direct evidence for such a pool of open unemployment among new in-migrants, since there is no data in the Census on unemployment by place of birth, let alone by duration of residence in the city, but some of the facts brought out by Zachariah's study suggest very strongly that this hypothesis is true. Worker-population ratios were lower among migrants of less than one year duration of residence, and there seems to have been substantial out-migration of recent in-migrants—presumably of those who failed to find jobs. Since migrants were on the whole less well-educated than the native popu-lation, if any such pool of unemployed existed it would probably have been of less well-educated people.

Labour Force and Labour Supply

It must be re-emphasized here that the resident labour force of the city at one time is, in itself, a statistic of limited significance. First, there is the purely geographical point that the number of workers in the city exceeds the number of resident workers; large numbers of commuters come in daily from outside the city boun-daries. Nor is there any reason to suppose that all those who are looking for jobs in the city are residents. Second, the city's labour force is not a hard datum independent of economic influences. Po-tential labour supply may be related to income-earning opportu-nities in the city and so indirectly to the demand for labour itself. If sufficiently attractive opportunities presented themselves, some residents (housewives or able-bodied beggars) may enter the labour force. More importantly, the flow of migrants into the city may be encouraged. Third , the labour force of the city, actual or potential, is heterogeneous. One important aspect of this is that all persons available for some work need not be available for full-time work. To understand the dynamics of the city's employment problem we need to know a great deal about the types of work performed in the city's economy and the characteristics of the people who perform them. We undertake this task in the next chapter.

APPENDIX II.1

Households

The Census defined a household as 'a group of persons living in the same house and eating from the same kitchen unless the exigencies of work prevented them from doing so'. A household thus defined is not the same thing as a family; its members need not be related by kinship and can include guests, lodgers and domestic servants. Equally, there can be groups of people meaningfully described as families, not all of whom live in the same place. In 1961, the Census counted 803,023 such households in Bombay, with an average membership of 5.03 members. This did not quite account for all of the population : 53,000 others were living in institutions such as hotels, hospitals and barracks, and there is also the 'houseless population', pavement-dwellers, of whom 62,000 were counted.

Table II.9

Size of Household and Sex Composition in Sampled Households, Bombay, 1961

Persons per household	Percentage of :		Males per 1000 females
	households	persons	
All Sizes	100.00	100.00	1319
1	9.06	1.82	6706
2 and 3	25.74	13.15	1537
4, 5 and 6	39.73	39.40	1254
7, 8 and 9	18.60	29.00	1229
10+	6.87	16.63	1304

SOURCE : Greater Bombay Census Tables, B-XVII; based upon a 20 percent sample, whose representativeness is discussed in the text.

Some idea of the size, distribution and sex composition of the households can be gathered from information from a sample taken during the Census shown in Table II.9. The average household size in this sample was also very close to 5 persons. It showed 85 per cent of the sample population to be in the two-thirds of households with four or more members. The main point of interest, however, is the variations shown by this table in the sex ratios by household size.

The relatively even sex ratios in the households with four or more members suggest that these contain married couples and their children who can be thought of as more definitely settled in the city. Apart from the one-couple nuclear family, such households comprise many forms of joint family household, with additional couples of the same or of successive generations, and additional single adults. To a certain extent the 'unpaired' male migrants are also found in these households, staying with relatives or as lodgers (otherwise the sex ratios would be close to unity); however there are proportionately more of them among the smaller households, especially among people living on their own. To a lesser extent there appear to be more 'unpaired' males among the largest households. This could reflect the existence of another type of household —the group of adult males sharing accommodation, as such groups are often quite large. In a survey carried out in the early sixties by J.F. Bulsara, all-male 'chummeries' (accounting for $1\frac{1}{2}$ per cent of all households) had an average of 7.5 members, and 16 per cent of them had more than 11 members.[14]

The high proportion of males among small households raises another interesting point about the reliability of urban household samples. It may explain why the excess of males in the population is understated by the sample. It is more difficult to collect survey information from small households consisting entirely of working adults. The sex ratio in the sampled population was 1,319 but that of the household population was 1,465 (itself lower than that of the city's entire population, 1,507, because of the high proportion of males among the institutional and houseless population). Other sample surveys of households in the city have shown a lower ratio of males to females than the Censuses. The Economic Survey of Bombay City, carried out in the mid-fifties, showed a sex ratio of 1,159 males per thousand females in the sample families (or 1,194 when living-in servants are included), and the sex ratio of the families sampled by Bulsara was 1,211.[15]

Note on the Estimation of the Contribution of Migration to the Change in Population, 1961-71

The net increase in the city's population over the decade was 1.8 million. This can be broken down in two alternative ways. It consists of the net increase in the non-migrant population plus the net increase in the migrant population, or alternatively as natural increase (births minus deaths) and net migration (in-migration minus out-migration). Although by definition the migrant population cannot be added to by births, both populations could experience change due to mortality, in-migration or out-migration. There were approximately 1.8 million births in the city during the decade.[16] The contribution of net migration to the city's population must have been almost the same as the number of deaths which occurred in the decade. We have attempted to measure the deaths one would have expected to occur in the city during the decade from using estimates of death rates[17] and the information about the age-structure of the population in 1961. Table II.10 summarizes our calculations.

This exercise suggested that the population in the city at the beginning of the decade had overall an 88.8 per cent chance of surviving until 1971, and that there would therefore have been about 465,000 deaths in this population. The 1,843,000 babies born during the decade had a somewhat lower chance of surviving, given the high mortality of infants and children in India, and according to the life-table might have accounted for as many as 376,000 deaths. These calculations suggest that the total number of deaths was about 841,000.[18] By subtracting deaths from births we arrive at an estimate of net natural increase in the decade as roughly a million (1,000,000). This leaves 819,000 of the change in population to be accounted for by net migration.

We have also made a rough estimate of the gross flow and of out-migration. The mortality rates and birth figures enable us to estimate what the expected size of the non-migrant population would have been in 1971 if there had been zero net migration among the native population. This produces an estimate of the population of migrants in the city's population in 1971 which is fairly close to that obtained in the CIDCO survey of 1500 households in the city during that year. The close similarity between the figures does not so much confirm the generalizibility of the survey results to the whole population as might appear, for there is almost certain to have been some net out-migration by natives which should make actual non-migrants fewer than pojected. However, the male natives in the survey are an even higher proportion of the population than those projected. Nevertheless the survey is consistent with the expectation that the share of city born in total population, as well as its increase, had risen, and suggests that this was not only due to an acceleration in the rate of addition to the population through births but also to a drop in the flow of in-migration. It would take fairly drastic revision of the survey information for these conclusions not to hold.

Table II. 10

Estimates of Decade-Change in Bombay's Population

	thousands	
	1951-61	1961-71
1. Change in total population	1158	1819
2. Net migration	600	819
3. Natural increase	558	1000
4. Gross migration	1202	1142
5. Out-migration	602	323
6. Out-migration by migrants	478	246
7. Out-migration by non-migrants	124	77
8. Births	816	1465
9. Deaths	258	465
10. Deaths of migrants	216	330
11. Deaths of non-migrants	42	135
12. Change in migrant population	508	566
13. Change in non-migrant population	650	1253
14. Share of migrants in total population	64.2%	54.15%

DEFINITIONS

Migrant—enumerated but not born in Bombay.

Non-migrant—native of Bombay (some of Zachariah's estimates also cover the population born outside the Indian sub-continent).

Gross migration—all migrants enumerated at the end of the decade with less than 10 years duration of residence; it is therefore net of deaths and out-migration amongst those who arrived in the city during the decade but who were no longer there at the end of it. In-migration amongst non-migrants (i.e. return migration of natives) has been ignored, assumed zero.

Births—are additions to the native population during the decade *who survive till the date of enumeration*. They are net of deaths and out-migration during the decade. The latter is assumed to have been negligible.

Deaths—includes only those among the original population at the beginning of the decade. Deaths amongst native or migrant newcomers have already been netted out.

Table II.10 (cont.)

SOURCES AND COMMENTS

| | 1951-61 | 1961-71 |

row

1 Difference between census count in 1961 and Zachariah's estimate of the 1951 population within the municipal boundaries of 1961.

1 Difference between two census counts.

2 Zachariah, Table 3.3. An estimate derived from reconciling 3 independent methods.

2 Row 1 minus row 3.

3 Row 1 minus row 2.

3 Row 8 minus row 9.

4 Migrants with less than 10 years duration of residence, from the Special Migration tables.

4 Proportion of migrants with less than 10 years' residence (35.35%) × proportion of migrants in population (54.15%), both from CIDCO survey 1971, × total population from 1971 census.

5 Line 4 minus line 2. This is the 'reconciled' estimate appearing on p. 58 of Zachariah's book. It is considerably higher than the out-migration implied by his calculation in Table 5.7, where he compares expected survivors from the 1951 population with the actual population of 1961 where duration of residence in the city is greater than 10 years. The discrepancy could be explained by faulty reporting of age or duration of residence. Even Zachariah's lower figure for out-migration (approx. 500,000) would exceed our estimate for the next decade.

5 Line 4 minus line 2. Gross migration minus net migration. Out-migration is also identically equal to Expected Survivors of 1961 population minus actual survivors. The first term can be calculated as the 1961 population minus deaths (line 9), the second term as the 1971 population less natives aged less than 10 (line 8) and minus migrants of less than 10 years' duration of residence (line 4).

6 Zachariah, p. 48. Expected minus actual survivors of 1951 migrant population in 1961.

6 Expected survivors of 1961 migrant population minus actual survivors (2337– 2091). Source

1951-61   1951-61

row

7 Line 5 minus line 6.

8 Line 3 plus line 9. This results
in a higher estimate than the
native population aged 0-9 reported by the 1961 Census,
685,000. It is however very
likely that this age group
should have been under-
counted and also have been
subject to faulty age reporting.
Using figures from Veena
Soni's article for fertility, and
approximate Life Table survival rates (0.8 for those aged
0-1 and 0.9 for those aged 1-9
at the end of the decade) one
would have expected the number born during the decade and
surviving until its end to be
979,000, a number even greater
than the one we use. In the
case of those under one year of
age the unreliablility of the
Census appears even more
serious. The Census count was
94,000; we estimate 120,000
(116,000 registered births ×
1.2943 for under-registration ×
.8 survival rate).

9 Zachariah, Table 5.7, uses
some unidentified Life Table
to predict deaths among the
1951 population, given its
age and sex structure.

10 Zachariah uses a 90% decade

for the latter figure is CIDCO
survey.

7 Line 5 minus line 6.

8 This estimate for births in
Bombay during the decade
comes from Veena Soni's
article. It is based on births
registered plus a correction
for under-registration. It implies a fertility rate in 1961
already lower than that of All-
India (182 as against 195 per
thousand females aged 15-44)
which fell during the decade,
especially its later years,
which is probably attributable
to the success of the family-
planning programme.

9 Deaths among 1961 population
of Bombay predicted using a
hypothetical Life Table for
India, 1961, prepared by
Keyfitz and Flieger in *World
Population* (Chicago 1968).
Even if this is treated as a
reliable source, our method
may over-estimate deaths if
death rates have fallen during
the decade, or if mortality in
Bombay is lower than in the
rest of India.

10 Keyfitz and Flieger survival

1951-61   1961-71

row

survival rate for the migrant
population of 1951 (op. cit.
p. 47).

rates applied to the age and
sex structure of the migrant
population in 1961 gave a
survival rate of 87.6.

11 Row 9 minus row 10.

11 Row 9 minus row 10.
(Survival rate 90.1)

12 Migrants of 1961 Census minus
estimates, based on Zachariah's
book, of 1951 migrant population, namely, 72.1% of 2,994,
444 (op. cit., Tables 3.1 and 1.3).

12 Migrants of 1971 estimated
from survey data and Census
total, less Census count of migrants in 1961: 3233 minus
2667.

13 Row 1 minus row 12.

13 Row 1 minus row 12. Also
equal to natural increase of
native population (row 8–
row 11)+ net migration of
non-migrants (– row 7).

14 1961 Census.

14 1971 Survey estimate. The
questionable validity of applying this to the whole population also affects the reliability
of estimates made in lines
4, 5, 6, 7 and 12 above.

APPENDIX II.3

Estimates of the 1971 *Labour Force*

The estimates of the 1971 labour force given in Table II.5 are rough, illustrative figures based upon the presumption that the reported 1971 figure for workers must be less than the 1971 labour force would have been had 1961 definitions been used to measure it. The difference consists of the openly unemployed in 1971 plus those who would have counted as workers in 1961 but who did not in 1971. Although, for reasons discussed elsewhere in this book, the Live Register of the Employment Exchange does not give an accurate representation of those a census might have recorded as openly unemployed, the direction of the inaccuracy is clear—the Live Register figure is likely to understate the openly unemployed. So the difference between reported workers and the labour force must have been at least as great as the 65,000 males and 14,000 females on the Live Register in March 1971. The foregoing considerations gave a lower bound to our labour force estimates which were made with some further assumptions about participation rates.

We have assumed that there were two downward pressures on the over-all male labour participation rate, viz. a change in the age-structure away from working ages as the native-born increased their weight in the population and a fall in age-specific participation rates owing to increased full-time education. The particular figures here combine (i) the assumption that the proportion of males aged 15-59 in the total population continued the trend shown in Table II.4 and dropped from 69.6 per cent to 67 per cent over the decade, with (ii) the assumption that ratio of the male labour force to the male population aged 15-59 dropped from 93 per cent to 92 per cent. No great precision is claimed for these guesses but comparison with the reported decade growth of 30 per cent in the number of workers suggests that the estimated decade growth of 34 per cent in the labour force implied by our assumptions is of the right order of magnitude. An alternative method of estimating male workforce growth (as opposed to labour force growth) yields a figure of the same order of magnitude—namely plus 35 per cent. This is based on the suggestion that reported male workers in 1971 should be compared with those in 1961 who were within the age-group 15-59 on the ground that older and younger workers were most likely to be those with an ambiguous commitment to economic activity.

Our estimate of the small part of the labour force composed of women leaves their overall participation rate unchanged, because it was felt that the change in definitions must have excluded a fairly significant proportion of female workers, apart from 14,000 on the employment exchange register. The effect of demographic changes on the female age structure would probably have shifted the age structure away from adult age groups as in the case of males, but the order of magnitude would not have been so great since the age structure was not so skewed in the first place and there might also have been a rise within the adult female population of groups with higher propensities to enter the labour force, such as the highly qualified and the unmarried.

NOTES

1 For more details about the migrant population of Bombay see K. C. Zacha-riah, *Migrants in Greater Bombay* (Bombay 1968). This is an excellent and comprehensive analysis of the data on the subject provided by the 1961 Census. The Census definition of a migrant as anyone not born in his place of enumeration gives a very broad definition of a migrant. It implies nothing whatsoever about the motive, if any, for the movement. A serious difficulty may be that it could include fairly large numbers of people who were born outside Bombay because their mothers, though normally resident in Bombay, had followed the custom of going to their parents' homes, which would in many cases be outside the city, to give birth. A survey conducted in 1971 suggested that there were 10 per cent of the city's population (or 20 per cent of its 'migrants') who were migrants according to the Birth-place criterion, but lifetime residents of Bombay according to the Usual Residence criterion.

2 Migrants also accounted for most of the excess of males (of the last 3 columns of Table II.4). The small excess of males which remains among the non-migrant population is not surprising. The population at large in India is characterized by a female deficit, and one would also expect the native-born population of any limited area to have lost females through their out-migration at marriage, since the general practice is for women to leave their own place of birth at marriage.

3 They are not strictly rates of out-migration because, instead of relating a flow of migrants during a given period to the stock of population at origin, they relate the stock of people who had come to Bombay at various times in the past and remained there in 1961 to the stock of population left

behind. A closer approximation to a migration rate can be achieved by comparing the migrants reporting less than one year's duration of residence with the population at origin. The results of this exercise are not shown because the ranking between different sources of migration is hardly changed; the areas with the high representation in the city also tended to have higher one-year migration rates, although the variation in those rates was somewhat reduced by the greater weight of recent migrants in the contingents from outside Western India.

4 See P.M. Visaria, 'The Pattern of Out-migration from Coastal Maharashtra in India' (Bombay and Princeton Universities, mimeo, 1969).

5 The existence of some such corridors created by contact with previous migrants from the same origin was strongly suggested by a cross-section multiple regression analysis of migration data in *Census of India 1961* by Sudhir Anand—'Rural-urban Migration: An Econometric Study' (mimeo, Harvard University, May 1971). Almost the only significant explanatory variable he found for the rate of migration from rural areas to urban destinations in other states was the stock of migrants from that origin already at each destination.

6 An alternative interpretation of the figures—earlier return migration by females—does not accord with what is known about migration habits nor with the return migration rates calculated by Zachariah.

7 The city also gained population through extension of its boundaries before 1961, but Zachariah's exercise allows for this factor since his figures for population in the earlier years, reproduced here, include an estimate of the population of the areas which were subsequently added to the city through boundary changes. The analysis of net migration (i.e. number of in-migrants minus number of out-migrants) is done in terms of absolute numbers because it is not very illuminating to talk in terms of a *rate* of migration. The latter is a fraction with the whole population of the city as the denominator. There could be changes in the rate of migration due to changes in this denominator which were not themselves due to changes in the flow of migrants; e.g. a flow of migrants which would be sufficient to keep the rate of migration constant if there were no other sources of addition to the population, would not be sufficient to keep the rate of migration constant if the population was also accumulating due to natural increase.

8 It is not very surprising that deaths exceeded births at a time when the population consisted predominantly of adult males, although, undoubtedly, unhealthy conditions in slums and mills, and epidemics contributed to the high number of deaths.

9 Notwithstanding the probability that it is also associated with a continued rise in the proportion of females among migrants.

10 See 'Proceedings of the Indian Association for the Study of Population, Conference on the First Results of the *Census of India 1971*' (Delhi, November 1971) and J. Krishnamurthy, *Economic and Political Weekly*, January 1972.

11 Female work participation rates are described in more detail in P.M. Visaria, 'The Level and Pattern of Work Participation in Greater Bombay' (Bombay University, mimeo, 1969).

12 *Asian Drama* (London, 1972), p. 1131.

13 Four occupational categories alone—domestic servants, general labourers, teachers and textile operatives—accounted for just over half of all female workers in 1961, or 21, 13, 9 and 7 per cent respectively. The corresponding percentages of male workers in these occupations were 5, 15, 1 and 11.

14 Cf. J. F. Bulsara, *Patterns of Social Life in Metropolitan Areas* (Research Programmes Committee, Planning Commission, Government of India, Bombay, 1970).

15 Cf. D.T. Lakdawala *et. al.*, *Work, Wages and Well-Being in an Indian Metropolis*, *Economic Survey of Bombay City* (Bombay University Press, 1963).

16 This estimate is taken from Veena Soni, 'Impact of the Family Planning Programme in Greater Bombay', *Economic and Political Weekly*, vol. VI, No. 35, 28 August 1971. It is based upon registered births multiplied by a factor of 1.2943 to adjust for under-registration as estimated in the early sixties. If registration had improved the actual number of births has been overestimated.

17 From a Hypothetical Model Life Table calculated for *India 1961* (Publications Division, Government of India) by N. Keyfitz and W. Flieger, *World Population: An Analysis of Vital Data* (Chicago, 1968).

18 We have ignored the possibility of deaths among migrants arriving after 1961, but we have also included deaths among 1961 residents who moved away from the city before dying. These two factors would not be large and will come close to cancelling each other out. The out-migrants have higher average age and therefore higher mortality, but there are fewer of them than in-migrants.

CHAPTER THREE

THE ANATOMY OF ECONOMIC ACTIVITY

This chapter begins by distinguishing between organized and unorganized activities, a distinction which we believe to be crucial to an understanding of the employment problem. It then proceeds to apply this distinction to the city's economy, making empirical estimates of the size and growth of the city's organized and unorganized workforce. It also discusses in some detail the composition of each of these sections of the workforce. To anticipate the argument of the later chapters, the trends considered below are very disturbing when viewed against the background of the highly privileged position of the organized sector.

A. THE DISTINCTION BETWEEN ORGANIZED AND UNORGANIZED ACTIVITIES

The city's economy can only be properly understood by making the vital, though rough, distinction between its organized and unorganized sectors. We discuss below several contrasting characteristics of the two sectors. Every enterprise would not necessarily possess all the characteristics of the sector to which it belongs but it would possess most of them. The characteristics can be grouped under three main headings: market structure, technology and relationship with Government.

Market Structure: The privately-owned part of the organized sector typically contains large manufacturing firms operating in oligopolistic markets sheltered from foreign competition by high tariffs and quantitative restrictions, selling their products mainly to middle and upper income groups. The unorganized sector contains a very large number of small producers operating on narrow margins in highly competitive product markets, selling a variety of goods and services. Its products are sold mainly to low income groups (though there are obvious and significant exceptions such as domestic service). The barriers to international trade do not help this sector nearly as much as they do the organized sector whose products are much better substitutes for imports and which receives much more effective protection, as a result of being favoured by the licencing system.

A salient feature of the organized sector is its relatively protected workforce. Strong trade unions negotiate on behalf of their members for higher wages and other benefits. Furthermore, workers are covered by reasonably effective labour legislation which lays down certain minimum standards of safety, medical attention, security of tenure, legal redress and so on. The unorganized sector consists partly of small firms which hire workers on a highly competitive casual labour market. However, it also contains a substantial amount of household employment and self-employment. This is an important contrast for certain purposes; for example, the supply price of labour may be lower for household enterprises than for capitalist firms because workers in the former share in the profits and may also be moved by family sympathy. However, especially in the urban context, it makes sense to lump the two together and contrast them with organized sector enterprises. In the unorganized sector, incomes are not protected; legal regulation of employment and wages is almost non-existent and extremely difficult to enforce where it does apply.

In the credit market, unorganized producers often have to rely on lenders who charge very high interest rates, perhaps partly to cover their risks but also, at least in part, because of the borrowers' low bargaining power. Organized sector firms, on the other hand, have greater access to the cheaper credit provided by the modern banking sector.

The remarks made above about private firms in the organized sector also apply in many respects to public sector activities except that little of their output is internationally traded. They should certainly be included in the organized sector.

Technology : Firms in the organized sector use mainly capital-intensive, imported technology in contrast to producers in the unorganized sector who use mainly a labour-intensive, indigenous technology. Labour productivity therefore is much higher in organized sector firms and the products are relatively more sophisticated. It has been asserted that the productivity of capital is also higher in many 'modern' enterprises and that 'traditional' producers use inferior techniques. This may be true in some cases because of scale economies and because systematic research and development activity is restricted to organized sector firms. However, it is unlikely to be generally true.

Technology in the organized sector demands routinized and formalized work conditions, greater division of labour and more sophisticated management. This in turn creates the possibility of process-workers acquiring training and of staff rising up a career ladder. The work situation in the unorganized sector is much more informal. Labour turnover is high and the employers themselves may often have less of a permanent identity. Impermanence or absence of formal organizations in the unorganized sector makes it easier for both the Government and the trade union movement to ignore it.

Relationship with Government : The relatively privileged position of the organized sector firms arises in large measure from their access to and influence over the machinery of Government. They can influence the allocation of import licences, investment licences and quotas of scarce materials. On the other hand, producers in the unorganized sector receive little direct help. The bureaucratic procedures which have to be followed to obtain scarce inputs, such as foreign exchange, are complicated enough to put them at a serious disadvantage or force them into riskier black-market transactions. Organized sector firms often employ people (graphically known as 'contact men') to deal with the bureaucracy and they have political pressure groups operating on their behalf. Unorganized producers, on the other hand, have little or no political 'pull'.

B. THE ORGANIZED AND UNORGANIZED SECTORS IN THE ECONOMY OF BOMBAY

One of our primary aims is to show that the unorganized sector employs a very substantial proportion of Bombay's workforce and to discuss the policy implications of this. The family of criteria discussed above cannot easily be used for empirical investigation. We think, however, that of these criteria, the size of establishment is a good and workable one for distinguishing between the sectors in practice. Most establishments employing large numbers of workers have organized sector characteristics; most establishments employing small numbers of workers do not. The next question concerns the employment size which would serve as a useful dividing line. Since the Directorate of Employment and Training collects data on the organized sector, defined as all public sector establishments and all privately owned establishments with more than 25 employees, this is certainly a convenient dividing line to use and we decided to use it. Can it also be defended as serving our purpose well?

It is certainly a good dividing line for isolating those workers who are more or less effectively safeguarded by labour legislation. Some establishments employing less than 25 are also covered by some Government legislation, but the difficulty of implementing it in these quarters is so great that they can for all practical purposes be regarded as being outside its scope. As for workers' organizations, even if they exist in the smaller establishments, they are weak and ineffective. When we think of other organized sector characteristics, our criterion is almost certainly too generous in classifying firms as organized. The typical organized sector enterprise using advanced technology, producing sophisticated products in a seller's market and receiving favourable Government treatment is very likely to employ more than 50 workers. (It is true that there are some small non-manufacturing establishments, e.g. those offering certain professional services, which are very much part of the organized sector but there are very few of these.) Another reason why our criterion probably leads us to overestimate the size of the organized sector is that in some large firms 'labour on the rolls' includes temporary, casual or contract labourers who do not share the advantages of permanent workers. So, though there is in reality a continuum of organized sector characteristics which is not exactly correlated with the employment size of the productive units, we feel confident that the Directorate's definition of the organized sector provides a maximum estimate of employment in establishments we have described as 'organized'. From now on, we use an initial capital letter to refer to the establishments covered by the Directorate and an initial small letter when making general remarks about the abstract concept. The Unorganized workforce refers to all workers, other than employers, not employed by the Organized sector.

Table III.1 shows the composition and growth of Organized sector employment from 1951 to 1971. It will be seen that Organized sector workers constituted about half the city's workforce in 1961 and that this proportion has shown no sign of rising over the twenty-year period. The overwhelming majority of other workers are in the

Table III. 1

Organized Sector Employment, Greater Bombay, 1951-71

thousands

Employment in:	1951	1961	1966	1971
PRIVATE SECTOR				
Factories	358	458	523	531
Other	n.a.[a]	94	116	97[d]
Total	445[b]	552	639	638
PUBLIC SECTOR				
Union Government	55	67	88	90
State Government	28	41	57	61
Municipal Government	52	70	89	94
Banks	3	6	10	30
Railways	51	91	96	105
Port	18	25	27	
Life Insurance	n.a.	6	8	10
Other Quasi-Government	n.a.	24	38	
Total	215[b]	330	413	473
ALL ORGANIZED SECTOR ESTABLISHMENTS	660[b]	882	1052	1111
All Workers (Census)[c]	1304	1687	n.a.	2198

NOTES:
a) Figures for Shops & Establishments given in the source are not used here as they appeared to cover many small establishments and family workers.
(b) Based upon a very rough estimate of missing categories of Organized workers.
(c) Note changes in Census definition of workers. The 1951 figure should be roughly comparable with 1961. It includes secondary earners and all major earners except those with unproductive sources of income. The 1971 definition is more restrictive. The Census in any case only covers workers resident in the city. Organized sector employees include some non-residents. The difference between the last two lines therefore understates the number of workers outside the Organized sector.
(d) Note the effect of Bank nationalization in 1969.
Sources: 1951—D.T. Lakdawala *et al.*, *Economic Survey of Bombay City*(Bombay 1963), ch. VIII; 1961, 1966 & 1971—Directorate of Employment, Bombay, Quarterly Returns, 1961, 1966 & 1971.

Unorganized sector, employers being small in number as we shall see below. As for the composition of the Organized sector work-force, a substantial but diminishing majority is to be found in the private sector. Of these, more than four-fifths work in factories, the rest are mainly employed in offices. The public sector workforce, shown as working for Central, State and Local Governments in-cludes not only those engaged in administration but also those in social services, communications, transport and public utilities as well as a small contingent in public sector manufacturing. Some im-portant public employers are specifically listed.

The size of the Organized sector was of the same order of magni-tude as that of the unionized labour force in 1961. Registered trade unions in that year claimed a membership of 703,542 in the city.[1] Data is not sufficiently detailed to show the industrial affiliation of union membership nor its overlap with Organized sector employ-ment but we expect the latter to have been very substantial.

C. ORGANIZED AND UNORGANIZED SECTOR EMPLOYMENT IN BOMBAY, 1961

Table III.2 shows the detailed breakdown of the city's resident workforce in 1961 into employers, Organized workers and Unorga-nized workers. As explained in detail in Appendix III.1, these are somewhat rough estimates based on data from the Census and from the Directorate of Employment and Training.

The Table shows the importance of Organized and Unorganized labour in different industry divisions. Primary activities fall almost entirely outside the Organized sector; the majority of workers in manufacturing are in the Organized sector and both sectors have substantial representation in Construction and Utilities, Transport, Services and Trade in ascending order of the relative importance of the Unorganized sector. Manufacturing is the biggest division of the city's workforce but only the third biggest division of Un-organized labour. The largest divisions of Unorganized workers are in services and trade which have second and third places in the overall ranking of divisions. Transport is the next biggest division in both sectors and the remaining divisions (Construction and Utilities, Agri-culture and Fisheries, Mining and Quarrying) are all much smaller.

More than half the Organized employees are to be found in Manu-facturing, of which a further three-fifths (more than 250,000) are in textiles. In manufacturing sub-divisions other than textiles, the Organized and Unorganized sectors account for roughly equal numbers of workers.

Organized workers in Transport and Communications are employed mainly in the public sector establishments connected with public transport, docks and shipping, postal services and telecommunications. In the Services division, while Unorganized workers not surprisingly predominate, the Organized sector is not negligible. However, the nature of the services provided is very different in the two cases. The Organized workers are mainly in Government administration, education and medicine, activities in which the public sector predominates. In the private sector they are employed in various professional and business enterprises, and in larger hotels and catering concerns. Nearly half the Unorganized workers are domestic servants; the rest perform a wide variety of petty services.

Some comment is in order on the data for Construction and Utilities which is very weak. The Organized sector figure for Construction exceeded the figure for employees given by the Census and the Organized sector figure for Public Utilities is smaller than that in the Census despite the fact that on our size criterion, one would expect all Public Utilities employment to have been within the Organized sector. We have not presented this implausible result. It is possible that some municipal workers associated with activities such as water-supply or sewerage but actually performing construction work were classified by the Census under Division 5 and by the Directorate under Division 4; hence we have lumped the two Divisions together. There was also the possibility that the Directorate's figure for Construction employees included some casual or contract workers who were classified by the Census as own-account or family workers. There is the further possibility that since many construction workers are temporary migrants with no fixed abode, they could have been under-enumerated by the Census. The major weakness of the segregation of these activities into organized and unorganized is that in these divisions, especially, it would be hard to maintain that all the workers reported by the Organized sector belonged to the sort of 'labour aristocracy' which, we argue, the Organized sector represents. The Utility workers include the low caste sweepers and scavengers, whose pay may in some cases be ensured by the municipality, but whose social status is far from aristocratic.

Similarly, in Construction, most of the unskilled work is performed by migratory gangs from Andhra on a casual labour basis for a daily wage which is relatively low. On analytical grounds, we should exclude all such labour from the Organized sector. The point made earlier that our estimate of the size of the Organized sector is a *maximum* estimate applies with particular emphasis here.

D. THE UNORGANIZED SECTOR IN BOMBAY, 1961

We have estimated the size of the Unorganized sector as the residual left after subtracting workers in all establishments employing more than 25 people from the total workforce. As for the Unorganized sector itself, nearly half of its members are own-account workers, unpaid family workers or workers in household industry. Of the 445,000 wage employees, about 100,000 are employed directly by households as servants and cooks, and the rest, 345,000 of them, typically work in very small establishments indeed, employing on average about four workers each. This is evident from the fact that there are 96,000 'employers' according to the Census, defined as persons at work who regularly hired other workers to assist in that work; on the other hand there are only 2,325 private establishments in the Organized sector, according to the Directorate, and we can assume that these establishments account for approximately one employer each. Thus, there were about 93,500 employers in the Unorganized sector hiring 345,000 workers—about four employees per employer. Table III.2 shows that there are variations within the Unorganized sector in this respect. In retail trading, for example, the ratio of employees to employers is less than two. As for manufacturing, though the average ratio is more than four, further examination shows that most of the units are again very small, as in retail trade. There are 27,500 employers in manufacturing as a whole. Of these, 1,400 are accounted for by Organized sector factories and about 2,500 by small but registered factories employing 10-25 workers each and employing in the region of 50,000 workers.[2] This leaves about 23,500 employers employing about 72,000 workers, i.e. about 3 workers per employer.

We now take a closer look at the composition of the Unorganized sector. Services (Division 8) account for 226,500 workers, or about 30 per cent of the Unorganized sector workforce. Of these 100,000 work for middle and upper income families providing domestic ser-

vices of various kinds. Some of these workers work full-time for
their employers and may lodge with them; others work part-time for
several employers. Given the prevailing social practice, the income
elasticity of demand for domestic service is high and most households would want to employ domestic help for menial tasks if they
can possibly afford to. The rest of the workers in this Division provide an astonishingly wide range of personal services characteristic of a less developed economy. There are about 13,000 *dhobis*
and about 11,000 barbers. Very few of these can afford to own premises. They solicit custom by going from door to door and through
contacts and build up clienteles in particular localities. *Dhobis* may
also work for laundries on a contract basis, washing clothes at
ghats and drying them in the sun. Barbers may perform their services under the shade of a tree. As for the other occupations, workers in small hotels and in catering are numerically quite important,
numbering about 50,000. The existence of a film industry in Bombay
creates many job-opportunities, though of a very irregular kind,
for film extras to appear in crowd scenes. There are many other personal services too various to mention in detail. Priests and astrolo-
gers, shoeshiners, masseurs, private tutors, self-appointed car-atten-
dants, snake-charmers, street dancers and acrobats—the list is
almost endless because necessity drives people to create work in
every conceivable way. Many of those in these occupations might
be on the margin of being beggars and probably shift between
begging and some activity of ambiguous value or legality to earn a
living.

There are 200,000 Unorganized workers in Trade and Commerce
(Division 6), about four times the number of Organized workers.
The majority are in retail trade rather than wholesaling or commerce
—small shopkeepers and hawkers working on their own account or
the employees of small shopkeepers. Nearly half of these sell food,
drink or tobacco. Fresh foods such as vegetables, milk, fish and,
less conspicuously, meat may sometimes be offered for sale by
members of a farming or fishing family that produce them but they
are also handled in big markets from which other hawkers operate,
taking baskets of fruit or vegetables to sell at street corners or from
door to door. The typical shop sells somewhat more durable goods
such as groceries, *pan* or cloth, but is still a fairly small-scale operation, run by its owner with perhaps one or two assistants. These
shopkeepers are generally licenced. Hawkers, who have no fixed

premises and smaller stocks spread their wares on pavements or carry them around on their heads or in ramshackle vehicles. They need a licence to operate but there are many unlicenced vendors who remain in business making some informal 'arrangements' with the police. There are also traders in all manner of lines, from scrap, second-hand goods, stolen and smuggled goods to manufactured novelties, who vary in extent of prosperity, scale of operation and degree of legality.

Contrary to a superficial conventional view, almost as many Unorganized workers are to be found in Manufacturing (Division 2) as in Services. The majority of workers are employees (122,000), but there is also a substantial number working on their own account (42,600), or as family workers (6,600) or as workers in household industry (22,900). As argued earlier a majority of the employees work in very small establishments. In our view, the manufacturing component of the Unorganized sector is of considerable economic importance, being a respository for many different types of skills. A few remarks are in order on some of the sub-divisions of Manufacturing listed in Table III.2. The Tobacco workers mostly produce indigenous cigarettes (*bidis*); more than two-thirds of them are non-employees and a high proportion of them are women. The Textiles sub-sector accounts for more than 27,000 workers of whom about 4,000 are engaged in making cotton cloth by hand spinning, hand-loom weaving or simple power-loom techniques. Garment-making is very largely an Unorganized activity carried on by tailors working in small shops; about 20,000 of them are to be found in this sub-sector. In this sub-sector, as in Tobacco, more than two-thirds of the workers are non-employees. On the other hand in most of the other sub-divisions the vast majority of the workers are employees. The workers in the Petroleum and Rubber products sub-division are engaged mainly in retreading tyres and manufacturing various rubber goods such as india rubbers; in the Chemicals sub-division they work mainly at producing soap, matches and common salt; in the Non-metallic products sub-division they produce principally building materials (such as bricks, tiles and dressed stones), pottery and miscellaneous glass products such as bangles and ornaments. The Metals and Engineering sub-division accounts for 41,000 workers, three-fourths of whom are employees. This sector is largely auxiliary to larger scale industry; bicycle and motor repair is an important activity, but it also covers the processing and manufacture of a wide

Table III.2

Estimated Employment in the Organized and Unorganized Sectors by Major Industry Divisions and Selected Industries, Greater Bombay, 1961

'000

Census Code	Industry	ORGANIZED EMPLOYEES	UNORGANIZED SECTOR			EMPLOYERS	TOTAL WORK FORCE
			Total	Employees	Others		
		(1)	(2)	(3)	(4)	(5)	(6)
0 & 1	PRIMARY PRODUCTION	0.5	30.1	15.9	14.2	1.4	32.0
2 & 3	MANUFACTURING of which:	466.7	194.3	122.1	72.2	27.5	688.5
20&21	Food & Beverages	14.5	10.4	6.5	3.9	1.9	
22	Tobacco	2.3	7.9	2.2	5.6	0.6	
23-27	Textiles	267.7	27.6	7.7	19.9	6.3	
30	Printing	14.7	8.0	6.8	1.2	2.0	
32	Petroleum	11.2	5.4	5.0	0.4	0.4	
33	Chemicals	29.4	11.5	9.6	1.9	2.4	
34-35	Non-Metallic Minerals	13.2	9.1	7.3	1.8	0.5	
36-38	Metals & Engineering	95.5	41.0	31.5	9.5	7.6	
28, 29 31 & 39	Miscellaneous	18.2	73.3	45.4	27.9	5.8	
4 & 5	CONSTRUCTION AND UTILITIES	57.3	14.2	2.3	11.8	2.5	73.9
6	TRADE AND COMMERCE of which:	56.0	200.3	88.0	112.3	47.5	303.8
60-63	Wholesale Trade	16.8	18.8	7.7	11.1	8.5	
64-68	Retail Trade	5.0	173.8	80.3	93.5	23.6	
69	Finance & Commerce	34.3	7.7	0	7.7	5.4	

		1	2	3	4	5	6
7	TRANSPORT AND COMMUNICATIONS	101.2	85.5	44.6	40.8	2.6	189.3
8	SERVICES	154.5	226.5	170.7	55.8	14.7	395.7
	of which:						
80	Public Administration	*81.9*	*0*	*0*	*0*	*0*	
81	Education	*31.0*	*1.2*	*0.1*	*1.1*	*0.7*	
82	Medicine	*9.5*	*11.4*	*8.5*	*2.9*	*1.8*	
88	Personal Services	*8.2*	*174.5*	*142.4*	*32.1*	*9.4*	
83-87 &89	Other Services	*23.9*	*39.4*	*19.7*	*19.7*	*2.8*	
9	Unclassified	1.3	2.0	1.3	0.7	0.1	3.5
	TOTAL	837.6	752.3	444.9	307.4	96.0	1686.7

NOTES

Column 1: Employees in the Public Sector and Private Sector establishments employing more than 25, including identifiable military personnel and excluding identifiable non-residents.

Column 2: Column 3 and Column 4.

Column 3: Difference between 'Employees in Non-Household Industry' given by the Census and Column 1.

Column 4: Single workers, family workers, workers in Household Industry, Cultivators and Agricultural Labourers as reported in the Census.

Column 5: Employers as reported by the Census.

Column 6: Total workers reported by the Census. Sum of Columns 1, 2 and 5.

SOURCES

Census of India 1961, vol. X, pt. X (1-B), Greater Bombay Census Tables: Primary Census Abstract, and Table B-IV, pts. A, B and C.

Directorate of Employment, Bombay, Quarterly Returns, December 1961.

See Appendix III.1 for a description of adjustments which had to be made to reconcile the two sources. Notes on individual rows in the Table follow general remarks.

range of metal and electrical goods and components in backyard
workshops. In the Miscellaneous sub-division, Wood Products
(Division 28) and Leather Products (Division 31) account for about
35,000 workers. The residual division (39), includes workers engaged in jewellery-making and repair, watch-repair and the production of items of stationery such as pencils and fountain-pens.

Two salient features of the Unorganized workforce in manufacturing may be noted. First, it is clear that the ratio of non-wage
labour to wage employees is higher in the more traditional industries
such as tobacco, textiles, leather and food-preparations; in the more
modern industries, the mode of production favours hired labour.
Second, the Unorganized sector is not entirely composed of extremely unskilled people. There is a very wide range of skills present
and there is reason to believe that the low incomes earned are the
result of lack of resources rather than of skill, effort or enterprise.

Unorganized labour in the other Divisions will be described more
briefly. In Transport and Communications we estimated 85,000
workers, half of whom are wage employees. This division comprises
the lorry-drivers and 'cleaners' who operate the many 'Public Carriers' that are to be seen on Indian roads, taxi-drivers, scooter-rick-
shaw-drivers, *mathadis* or head-load carriers, other coolies, porters and loaders and the small army of tiffin-carriers who operate
an intricate city-wide system to bring meals to workers from their
homes. The Construction and Utilities division accounts for only
14,000 workers, mainly building labourers according to Table
III.2, but for reasons explained earlier, this figure is suspect and
almost certainly an underestimate. This leaves only the Primary
industries with 30,000 workers of whom about 8,000 are fishermen.

An important group of activities which we have not discussed
so far consist of those which are regarded as 'non-economic' by
the Census, following usual conventions. Begging, for example,
is regarded as receiving a transfer payment rather than an economic
activity though it involves some effort for the beggar and provides
him with an income (and, conceivably, the beggar also provides a
service if he makes the charitable man feel good). Illegal and cri-
minal activities such as thieving, robbery, bootlegging and smuggling are also regarded as non-economic; so is prostitution which
is not illegal but is disapproved of by the established ethic. Without
doubt, many people in Bombay earn their livelihoods in these ways.
If they declared themselves to be doing one of these

would not be counted by the Census as part of the labour force. Very likely, many of them declare themselves as doing something legal, which they may well be for part of the time. Legal and illegal, economic and non-economic activities shade into each other easily and it is very possible that numbers of people derive incomes from more than one type of activity. The Census enumerated about 10,000 beggars but this is probably an underestimate. Estimates of the number of the prostitutes in the 1950s range from 7,000 to 15,000, so they could easily add 10 per cent to the conventionally defined female workforce.

Bombay is a major centre of the 'black money' or 'parallel' economy, which comprises the entire range of illegal and unofficial activities from bootlegging and smuggling to bribery and tax evasion, partly because of the traffic in smuggled gold in which many people try to hold their illegal assets. The 'parallel' economy provides income in a big or small way for many citizens, a number of whom are attached to the Organized sector, besides supplementing sources of income outside it.

E. GROWTH OF THE ORGANIZED SECTOR, 1961-71

(a) *The Overall Picture*: Table III.1 shows that Organized sector employment as a proportion of Bombay's workforce did not increase between 1951 to 1971. Figures for 1951 are rather uncertain and not suitable for detailed comparisons; one can, however, be more precise about the period 1961-71. Organized employment grew fairly steadily in the first half of the sixties. After 1966 there was a period of stagnation and recession which hit employment in private manufacturing particularly hard. Though growth picked up somewhat towards the end of the sixties, the increase in Organized employment over the decade as a whole was only 26 per cent. During the same period the change in total numbers at work must have been at least as great as the 30 per cent difference between the two Census counts of workers—which itself is an under-estimate on consistent definitions. The increase in the labour force was 34 percent according to our estimates in Ch. II. Thus, not only have the number of workers outside the Organized sector in the city remained substantial, they have increased both absolutely and as a proportion of the labour force. In a period when the city's population increased by nearly 2,000,000 and the labour force by about 600,000, there

Table III.3

Growth of Urban Population and Employment, Greater Bombay and Thana District

	1961	1966	1967	1968	1969	1970	1971	decade difference %
Greater Bombay								
1. Population	4152						5969	43.8
2. Workers: Censuses	1687						2198	30.3
3. Workers: Organized	883	1046	1041	1036	1039	1078	1111	25.8
4. Manufacturing: Censuses	689						930	35.0
5. Manufacturing: Organized	467	536	539	527	527	556	571	22.3
Thana District Urban Areas								
6. Population	499						827	65.7
7. Workers: Censuses	173						270	57.9
8. Workers: Organized	53	97	110	123	131	142	147	177.8
9. Manufacturing: Censuses	66						126	91.4
10. Manufacturing: Organized	36	65	73	37	95	105	108	201.9
Bombay and Thana Combined								
11. Population	4651						6796	46.1
12. Workers: Census	1859						2468	32.8
13. Workers: Organized	936	1143	1151	1159	1170	1220	1258	34.4
14. Manufacturing: Censuses	754						1056	39.9
15. Manufacturing: Organized	502	601	613	613	622	661	678	35.0

NOTES:

1. *Geographical coverage.* The Census figures for Thana district refer only to urban areas, but there is no guarantee that the Organized sector figures are confined to establishments located in municipal areas, nor that their employees reside in urban areas. The presumption is that the bulk of Organized employment is urban (in both these senses) so that the comparison made here was more meaningful than one with the Census figures of workers in both rural and urban areas of the district.

2. *Census reports of workers* (lines 2, 6 and 10). The criterion used by the Census to identify workers was altered in 1971 to become more conservative. The decade-change observed is an under-statement of employment growth on consistent definitions. The adjustment should probably be an upward revision in the region of about 5 percentage points.

3. *The Organized sector in Thana District.* The Directorate of Employment only started collecting information in Thana at the end of 1965. The figures have a wider establishment coverage than those for Bombay, since these cover all private establishments employing more than 10, and also include some smaller ones. Unlike Bombay, these figures have approximately the same coverage of manufacturing as the Factory Act Returns. Our figures for Thana in 1961 are rough estimates based upon Factory Act data. To estimate 1961 manufacturing employment in Thana, firstly employment in non-manufacturing activities covered by the Factory Act (electricity generation, laundries, etc. 1,397), was subtracted from the total average daily employment in factories in 1961 (35,399). The remaining figure will probably be lower (as it was in 1966-7) than the estimate that would have been made by the Directorate because (i) average daily employment (recorded by the Factory Act) is expected to be lower than labour on the rolls on a given day (recorded by the Directorate) as the former excludes absentees, and (ii) the Factory Act figures exclude some managerial staff. The Factory Act figure was thus increased by an arbitrary 5 per cent to estimate manufacturing employment equivalent to the Directorate's 'Organized sector'. To estimate total Organized sector in 1961, the figure for manufacturing thus estimated was multiplied by the ratio of total Organized employment to manufacturing in 1966.

SOURCES:

Lines 1, 2, 4, 6, 7, 9, 11, 12, and 14, *Census of India 1961* and *1971*, Maharashtra General Population Tables.
Lines 3, 5, 8, 10, 13 and 15, mainly Directorate of Employment—see note 3.

were only about 250,000 additional jobs in the Organized sector.

An important qualification must be discussed here. During the sixties, the metropolitan economy was expanding rapidly on adjacent areas of the mainland, outside the municipal limits but within the Metropolitan Region. Expansion of employment within the city was affected not only by the industrial recession but by Government policy of discouraging industrial location inside the city and also by the fact that industry in the city is weighted heavily towards textiles which were particularly stagnant. The best available approximation to the employment figures for the part of the Metropolitan Region beyond the city limit are figures for Thana district where the Directorate started collecting information in the mid-60s.[3] Bringing in figures for Thana District as a proxy for the rest of the Metropolitan Region reverses the conclusion that manufacturing has been a lagging part of the Organized sector and it weakens, though it does not overturn, the conclusion that demand for labour by the Organized sector failed to keep pace with the growth of the labour force. On the first point, it will be seen from Table III.3 that during the second half of the decade, when Organized employment, and particularly manufacturing, was in recession in Bombay proper, it was expanding very fast in Thana. From 1966 to 1970 there were only 32,000 new jobs in Bombay, an addition of 3 per cent over 4 years, while Thana gained 45,000 jobs, an increase of over 45 per cent. Of the additional jobs, manufacturing accounted for 20,000 in Bombay and 40,000 in Thana. In the combined districts factory employment grew faster than the rest of the Organized sector both in the second half of the decade and, as far as we can tell, over the whole ten year period. On the second point, we compare Organized sector growth in the combined districts with data on demographic changes. We see from Table III.3 that Organized sector employment in the combined districts grew at an estimated 34 per cent over the decade while the urban working population grew by something more than 33 per cent. If the excess of the 'true' change in the labour force over the recorded change in the number of workers in the combined areas is about the same as we calculated for Greater Bombay, viz. an additional 4 per cent, the metropolitan labour force must have grown by 37 per cent.[4] Even with a fairly wide margin of error, this is greater than the increase in Organized employment.

It may be useful to compare the Bombay and Thana picture with

Table III.4

Organized Workers in Total Workforce: Bombay, Maharashtra and All India, 1971

millions

	Non-cultivating workers in urban areas	'Non-rural' Organized Employment	Percentage of Organized in workforce (2) ÷ (1)
	(1)	(2)	(3)
All India	28.44	14.77	51.9
Maharashtra	4.54	2.43	53.6
Bombay	2.20	1.08	49.1
Thana	0.27	0.14	51.9
Bombay & Thana	2.47	1.22	49.4

NOTES :

Column 1 Workers in urban areas as reported in the 1971 Census, excluding cultivators and agricultural labourers, who could not possibly be in the Organized sector.

Column 2 Organized workers in Plantations, Forestry, Mines and Construction have been excluded because these activities are more likely than others to be in rural areas. The All-India figures do not include Jammu and Kashmir and the smaller Union Territories where Organized employment is not reported.

SOURCES :

(1) *Census of India 1971*, Paper 3 of 1972 and Maharashtra—several Population Tables. (2) Directorate-General of Employment and Training, New Delhi, and Directorate of Employment, Bombay.

that of the share of the Organized sector in employment in other parts of urban India. As systematic data collection was starting up during the sixties, it only makes sense to do this for the second half of the decade. As shown in Tables III.4 and III.5 respectively, Bombay is not unique in having about half its workforce in the Organized sector, nor in experiencing relatively slow growth of Organized sector employment.

During the period 1966-71, Organized sector employment in All India expanded by 8 per cent. During the same period, the overall labour force was projected to increase by 12 per cent—approximately 2.4 per cent p.a. rising to 2.6 per cent p.a. during 1971-6.[5] In only one year did the rate of growth of Organized employment

Table III.5

Employment in the Organized Sector, All India, 1966-71

	1966	1967	1968	1969	1970	1971
millions						
All Industries	16.19	16.32	16.33	16.63	17.04	17.45
Non-rural Industries	13.37	13.58	13.72	14.02	14.41	14.77
Percentage change over previous year						
All Industries		0.8	0.1	1.8	2.5	2.2
Non-rural Industries		1.6	1.0	2.2	2.8	2.5

NOTE: 'Non-rural industries' as in Table III.4.
SOURCE: Director-General of Employment and Training, New Delhi·

exceed the projected trend rate of growth of the labour force. Another comparison, and possibly a more pertinent one, would be that of the growth of Organized *urban* employment with the growth of the *urban* labour force. We can approximate the former by excluding Primary industries and Construction.[6] When these industries are excluded, the growth of the Organized sector improves to 10 per cent but the growth of the urban labour force must have been higher than the 12 per cent growth of the overall labour force.[7] Thus, even if we exclude some of the more backward and sluggishly growing parts of the Organized sector, there are only two years when the increase in employment exceeds the projected trend rate of growth of the overall labour force (2.4 per cent) and none where it reaches the probable rate of growth of the urban labour force (3 per cent or more).

(b) *Some Aspects of Organized Sector Growth*: Noteworthy features of the changes within the Organized sector employment in Bombay were :

(i) the stagnation of employment in the cotton mills,
(ii) the relatively fast growth of the public sector and of skill-intensive industries, and
(iii) the changing activities of women workers.

A summary picture of the changing composition of organized employment in the sixties is given in Table III.6.

(i) *Stagnation of Cotton Mill Employment*

The cotton mills, the oldest established factory industry of Bombay, remained in 1961 by far the biggest employer of labour in manufacturing, accounting for half of all workers in manufacturing.

Earlier, this pre-eminence had been even more marked. During the sixties, the relative decline of cotton mill employment turned into an absolute decline. There was stagnation in output as well as replacement of men (and especially women) by machinery.[9] The latter phenomenon, known in the industry as 'rationalization', is probably in part a case of pure factor substitution in response to higher wage costs but probably also reflects changes in technique in response to changing product-mix and also pure technical progress. Superior techniques tend to involve increases in capital intensity and so do new types of cloth—synthetics and blends—as well as higher quality cotton textiles.

While India's cotton industry as a whole was losing ground on world markets, the decline in mill employment was more pronounced in Bombay than in the rest of the country. This was presumably because of the greater weight of high quality cloth in the output of Bombay cotton mills and because of the high level of wages in Bombay in relation to other parts of the country. As can be seen from Table III.6 the growth of employment was much faster in a newer industry like chemicals. Pharmaceuticals, accounting for half the decade increase in this industry, more than doubled. Other branches of manufacturing expanded employment at a rate comparable with other sectors of production. It should be pointed out that the skill-intensity of expanding industries such as petrochemicals, pharmaceuticals and electronics is probably significantly higher than that of the older, stagnating textile sector.

(ii) *The Faster Growing Sectors*

A striking feature of Organized employment growth in the sixties is the contrast between the public and the private sectors. Although at the end of the decade the private sector still remained the larger employer, employment in the public sector increased by about 43 per cent and that of the private sector by only 15 per cent. The private sector bore the brunt of the recession; employment fell between 1966 and 1968, and did not regain its 1966 level until 1971. Although the growth of the public sector slackened slightly during the same period it maintained its upward movement throughout. Even before 1966 the public sector grew faster than the private sector, by 24 per cent as against 15 per cent. It might be objected that the contrast given above is to some degree spurious in that it results from the bank nationalization of 1969 which resulted

Table III.6

Decade Change in Organized Sector Employment, by Industry and Sectors, Greater Bombay, 1961 to 1971

Code	Industry	Estimated Employment 1961 '000 (1)	Estimated Employment 1971 '000 (2)	Decade Change Absolute number '000 (3)	Decade Change Percentage increase (4)
0	AGRICULTURE, FISHERY etc.	0.3	0.4	0.1	27
1	MINING AND QUARRYING	0.2	—	-0.2	-97
2 & 3	MANUFACTURING	466.7	570.6	103.9	22
	of which				
232	Cotton Mills	229.0	226.3	-2.7	-1
33	Chemicals	29.4	52.9	23.5	80
36-8	Engineering	95.5	133.0	37.5	39
	Other manufacturing	112.8	158.4	45.6	40
4 & 5	CONSTRUCTION AND UTILITIES	57.3	53.3	4.0	-7
6	TRADE AND COMMERCE	61.8	79.8	-17.9	29
	of which				
690-8	Banking, Insurance, Commerce, etc.	40.1	56.8	16.7	42
7	TRANSPORT AND COMMUNICATION	156.7	199.5	42.9	27
8	SERVICES	139.8	207.3	67.5	48
	of which				
80	Public Administration	67.2	87.5	20.3	30
81	Education	31.0	58.8	27.7	89
82	Health	9.5	26.0	16.4	172
	TOTAL PUBLIC SECTOR	330.4	472.8	142.5	43
	TOTAL PRIVATE SECTOR	552.4	638.0	85.6	15
	GRAND TOTAL	882.8	1110.9	228.1	26

Table III.6 (cont.)

NOTE:

No attempt has been made to adjust these figures for non-residents or military personnel, hence 1961 figures are not identical with those in Table III.2.

Columns 3 and 4 calculated on the basis of unrounded figures.

SOURCE:

Directorate of Employment, Bombay, Quarterly Employment Returns and *The Bombay Labour Market*, 1966 in public sector employment growing at the expense of the private sector without there being any corresponding increase in overall employment. But our calculations show that if this shift in employment is ignored, the decade-growth in the private sector is 18 per cent and the decade-growth in the public sector is 39 per cent.[10] So the conclusions continue to hold. Within the public sector, government administration grew fast; however, the growth of the sector as a whole is not to be attributed merely to an over-luxuriant expansion of the bureacracy.[11] Notable is the very rapid expansion of employment in health and education which are predominantly in the public sector. Since one can reasonably assume that output in these sectors grew as fast as employment and since (according to Table II.5) the growth of the dependant population was about 50 per cent, we can surmise that per capita availability of health and education probably improved over the decade and that the proliferation of public sector employment in this direction has not been useless.

Table III.6 also points to the fact that those industries where employment expanded faster than average were also avenues for employment of the more educated. These avenues appear to have been in the 'office-going' or 'white-collar' industries of administration, finance, education and in the 'white-coated' industries like medicine and technology-based manufacturing. One has to be careful not to pay excessive attention to growth rates. Though manufacturing and transport grew slowly, they nevertheless accounted for well over half the new jobs in the Organized sector. Furthermore, to fully appreciate the employment potential of manufacturing, one must take into account the deliberate redirection of investment away from Greater Bombay towards the rest of the Metropolitan Region. Nevertheless, it is probably true that with the increasing sophistication of modern industry, the capacity of the Organized sector to absorb unskilled labour is diminishing.

(iii) Women Workers

These tendencies can be seen in an exaggerated form when one examines the trends in employment of the tiny proportion of women working in the Organized sector. Although it remained even smaller than the proportion of females in the total workforce, and the Organized sector still accounted for a minority of female workers, the share of women in Organized sector employment rose from 6 per cent in 1961 to 8 per cent in 1971. This represents an increase, from 53,000 to 88,000, of 66 per cent which is considerably higher than the 23 per cent in male Organized sector employment, but not so very much higher than the 50 per cent increase in the female population.

As will be seen from Table III.7 this increase was almost entirely attributable to a set of six industries which not only employed an atypically high proportion of women, but which mainly provided jobs for women with educational qualifications. Women employed in education are mainly teachers; in medicine, doctors and nurses; in pharmaceuticals, mainly packers; in post and communications, telephone operators. For both the latter jobs, educational qualifications of at least matriculate level are required, as also for office jobs in the civil service and in banking. In these six industries, which were anyway growing relatively fast, the employment of women more than doubled. The ratio of female to male workers increased, and the total number of female Organized employees accounted for by the six industries rose from 43 per cent to 63 per cent.

In contrast, the cotton mills, which had been the largest single employer of women in the Organized sector at the beginning of the decade, cut female employment by over 40 per cent. The women employed in the mills were largely unskilled and illiterate reelers and winders, whose tasks were becoming increasingly automated.

The case of the cotton mills provides an illustration of the thesis that social conventions put women at a disadvantage in the job market. Not only are women's jobs strictly confined to a few occupations (in other countries, a far higher proportion of textile workers are female), but in a situation where jobs are scarce, they find it particularly hard to compete with men. However, such a phenomenon does not appear to have prevented the share of women increasing in the parts of the Organized sector which employ skilled women. Employers' prejudices against female employees seem to have been breaking down. But there was probably also a particularly large increase in the numbers of educated women, and possibly in their propensity to seek work, making for a substantially faster growth of educated labour supply from females than from males. Despite the increases in jobs for educated women, the fastest growing item in Table III.7 is the number of female registered job-seekers. Educated women were probably not finding jobs any more easily than men.

The interpretation of Live Register data is discussed in Appendix III.2. Further details of the sex composition of the Organized sector nda Total Workforce are shown in Appendix III.3.

(c) The Labour Force Outside the Organized Sector, 1961-71

Besides Organized employees, the labour force includes employers, Unorganized workers and the openly unemployed. Information on developments among these categories is difficult to come by. An indication of unemployment is provided by the number of registered job-seekers on the Live-Register which more than doubled over the period, from 44,037 in December 1961 to 90,654 in December 1971. This indicates that open unemployment increased markedly. However, since the correspondence between the openly unemployed and the registered job-seekers is far from perfect, it is difficult to be precise about the exact change in open unemployment in absolute terms or as a proportion of the labour force. The 1961 Census counted 80,416 openly unemployed but the 1971 Census did not count them at all. Our guess is that unemployment as a proportion of the labour force was at least as high at the end of the decade as at the beginning, viz. between 4 and 5 per cent of the labour force—or at least 108,000. For details of the unemployment data and the conclusions therefrom, the reader is referred to Appendix III.2 at the end of this chapter. The information on open unemployment refers principally to those who are seeking entry into the Organized sector who are more likely than most to be educated. The phenomenon of educated unemployment is undoubtedly of considerable social and political importance but, as we have argued earlier, the 'employment problem' is far wider than that and the figures of open unemployment, even if they were available, would not by any means tell the whole of the story.

The rest of the story of course concerns the Unorganized workers. We have already shown that the workforce in the Unorganized sector was increasing rapidly in this period, as fast if not faster than the Organized workforce. The hasty conclusion that a proliferation of petty service activities acted as a sponge to absorb the excess labour is probably not entirely true. Preliminary data on the industrial composition of the 1971 workforce presented in Table III.8 shows that at least in manufacturing and trading the Unorganized sector grew faster than the Organized sector.[12] For other industrial divisions, the apparent faster increases of the Orga-

Table III.7

Women in Organized Sector Employment and among Registered Job Seekers, Bombay, 1961-71

	Women			Persons		
	thousands		percentage	thousands		percentage
	1961	1971	change	1961	1971	change
Selected industries employing educated women						
Education	10.2	20.6	+103	31	59	+89
Public Administration	4.0	10.4	+158	67	87	+30
Medicine	2.9	9.9	+235	10	26	+172
Commerce & Banking	2.5	6.3	+160	40	57	+42
Pharmaceuticals	1.9	4.4	+127	10	22	+116
Post & Communications	1.6	3.3	+145	17	29	+72
Sub-Total	23	55	+140	175	280	+60
Cotton Mills—*women mostly unskilled*	11	6.5	−41	229	226	−1
Other Organized Sector	19	26	+36	488	604	+24
TOTAL ORGANIZED SECTOR	53	88	+66	883	1111	+26
Employment Exchange						
Live Register—*women mostly educated*	4	14	+286	44	79	+88

SOURCE: Directorate of Employment, Bombay.

Table III.8

Workers Outside the Organized Sector, Greater Bombay 1971 and Comparison with 1961

Industry	1971 (thousands)			1971—1961 as % of 1961		Interpretation
	Workers reported in Census	Organized[b]	Non-Organized	Census counts[a]	Organized sector	
Primary Sector	28	1	27	−15	−25	} Negligible Organized Sector
Household Manufacturing	29	—	29	27	—	
Non-Household Manufacturing	900	571	329	35	2	} Unambiguous increase of Non-Organized
Trade & Commerce	492	78	413	62	38	
Construction	67	29	38	49	1	} Organized Sector figures subject to error
Transport & Communication	237	137	100	25	35	
Services & Public Utilities	446	276	169	4	50	Probable increase in Organized share notwithstanding note (a.).
TOTAL	2198	1091	1107	30	30	Probable relative increase of Non-Organized Sector.

NOTES: (a) True changes in numbers at work are understated because of changed definitions. Those excluded by new procedures are unlikely to have been in Organized employment. Hence increases outside the Organized sector are understated.

(b) Adjusted for comparability with Census

SOURCE: Appendix III.3.

nized sector may merely be the result of changed census definitions, but the apparent absolute fall in male service workers outside the Organized sector may actually reflect a fall in activities such as domestic service. Turning to the wider metropolitan economy, it will be seen from Table III.3, that even after the new factories of Thana are taken into account, the employment growth in Organized manufacturing was outstripped by the smaller scale sector. To the extent that the increased Unorganized workforce went into manufacturing activities, they may well have been employed productively.

F. SUMMARY

In this chapter we have attempted to give empirical content to the distinction between the organized and unorganized sectors. We have examined the size, composition and growth of these two sectors in some detail. We have shown that in Bombay, as elsewhere in India, unorganized workers constitute half the urban workforce and that they are increasing rapidly in numbers, as fast if not faster than organized workers. Before assessing the social and economic significance of these trends, we enquire into the relative incomes of the two groups of workers and into patterns of migration. The following two chapters are concerned with these questions.

Further Notes on Table III.2

(a) *General Remarks on the Estimation of the Unorganized Sector in 1961*

This estimate is based upon a comparison of two sets of not exactly comparable data, namely that from the Directorate of Employment and the Census. The exercise cannot claim great precision, but it can give an idea of rough orders of magnitude, and is therefore worth the trouble since we know of no other way of measuring the extent of this important phenomenon. In the first place the two agencies whose data we have used are not measuring exactly the same phenomenon. In the second place, the accuracy of measurement which is achieved, especially with figures from the Directorate, leaves a considerable margin of error. There is also no guarantee that the classification of individual workers by two different agencies into industrial or work-status categories would necessarily be identical.

The Directorate reports employment by work-place, the Census reports the industrial affiliation of workers by place of residence. The first difficulty with the comparison is that not all people working in the Bombay area reside there, and not all workers living in Bombay work within the city limits. Only if the net number of commuters in each industry were zero, could residence and work-place data give identical results. Although it is true that, at least by the end of the sixties, some residents of Greater Bombay were commuting to jobs outside the city limits in Thana district, it seems extremely probable that on balance in 1961 there was a net inflow of daily commuters, living outside the district but employed within it. Since the vast majority of such commuters are likely to be employed by the Organized sector, we can say that our method of estimating Unorganized employees—namely subtracting from resident employees the employees of large-scale establishments—will tend to understate the size of Unorganized employment. It is difficult to correct for this factor because we have only a very hazy notion of the numbers of such commuters and their industrial affiliation. On the latter question one can say that tertiary Organized employment, being concentrated in offices in the southern tip of the city, away from residential districts, is likely to involve more long-distance commuting, and therefore more commuting from outside Bombay, than industrial employment which is more evenly spread around the city. Furthermore, in so far as there are Bombay residents travelling to work outside Bombay, they are more likely to be involved in manufacturing than tertiary activities, given the predominance and growth of manufacturing in the Organized employment of Thana district. We have made allowances for what appear to be about 35,000 commuters employed in commerce and transport. We suspect that there were some more in-commuters working in other service industries but their number could have been cancelled out by people commuting out to Thana. On the question of the overall size of the flow of commuters, we have the evidence from a Transport Study[13] referring to 1968 that there was a net inflow of 33,000 workers commuting-in to Bombay (about 3 per cent of the Organized workforce). This involved 53,000 commuting-in to the Central Business District alone, and therefore at least 20,000 commuters-out. Since the number of commuters-out is likely to have grown at least as fast as the number of commuters-in between 1961 and 1968, we can say that there may have been a greater balance of non-resident workers in 1961 than we have allowed for. To the extent that this is the case we have underestimated the Unorganized sector, but we are more likely to have done so in tertiary industries than in manufacturing.

The second reason why the two sets of figures are not comparable is that the Directorate reports only civilian employment, while the Census reports the industrial affiliation of all residents including military personnel. It was possible to make allowances for those military personnel whom the Census classified as 'workers in government services' (div. 80) but not all military personnel are so classified. If they are engaged in some activity which is identifiable as another industry they are classified as such. Since we were not able to identify these military employees who should have been counted as employees of the Organized sector, our estimates of Unorganized labour will be overstatements to the extent that they include such people. The numbers involved would be a state secret, but one can guess that the order of magnitude involved could not have been more than 20,000. We have already identified some number smaller than 15,000 as the military personnel classified under division 80.

There is a third reason for non-comparability of data collected from residences and from work-places. This concerns the possibility that an individual may be employed in more than one establishment so that the Directorate of Employment would count him more than once, though the Census would count him only once and list him as being involved in the industry where he spent the major part of his time. There is no information on the extent of the phenomenon of 'moonlighting' in Bombay, but to the extent that it exists our estimate of the Unorganized sector is too low on a second count. The likelihood of many people holding two jobs both in the Organized sector is, however, rather small.

The major reason why the figures shown in the Table cannot be regarded as accurate is the poor quality of the data for 1961 from the Directorate. Although the scheme to record employment started in 1961, returns were only available for September and December and did not include any allowance for employment in non-reporting private sector establishments. The total for September which appears from these returns is 816,000. The Directorate has subsequently produced an estimate for employment in 1961 (month not stated) of 882,800 workers. This included allowances for employment in non-reporting establishments and establishments subsequently identified. The report[14] in which this estimate appeared did not give an industrial breakdown of this revised estimate; so we have made the following arbitrary assumptions in order to estimate the size of the Organized and Unorganized sectors in March 1961, the date of the Census. We have assumed that any information we have for 1961 (employment in reporting establishments, 30th September; industrywise distribution of non-reporting establishments, December; and an estimated overall total, undated, but probably referring to September) was approximately the same as data for March would have been. We have therefore taken the September figures for public sector employment as if correct for March and attributed the unreported 67,000 to the private sector of each industry in proportion to the number of non-reporting establishments and average employment per reporting establishment in each industry. It cannot be claimed that the estimates for Organized sector employment derived in this way are completely infallible but they should give a general idea of orders of magnitude. Having arrived at an Organized total of 882,800 by the process outlined above, further amendments to take into account identifiable non-comparabilities with the Census were made, as explained in the following notes on individual items in the Table.

(b) *Some particular items in Table III.2*

Divisions 0 & 1   Industry Division 0, Agriculture, Livestock, Forestry
 and Fishing, has been lumped together with Industry Division
 1, Mining and Quarrying, because of the small size of these
 divisions, especially div. 1.

Division 45   Construction and Utilities have been lumped together
 because, as discussed in the text, it is suspected that the Directorate classified as Construction workers, some of the workers
 classified by the Census under Public Utilities.

Division 69   Directorate-based estimates for div. 69 vastly exceeded
 Census employees in this category. The Directorate figure for
 div. 699, 'trade not elsewhere classified', which vastly exceeds
 the Census 699, was attributed to divs. 690-98, and the remaining
 excess of Organized over resident employees, 5,800, was assumed to be a minimum estimate for commuters working in
 this division. If there were more commuters, the figure for Unorganized employees should be greater than 0.

Division 7   Transport and Communications. The raw data from the
 Directorate gave more employees in the public sector alone
 (155,404) than the Census report of employees in this division
 (146,782). The following allowances were made on the basis of
 the 3-digit industrial classification of workers in the Census,
 and of employees in the Directorate figures. The Directorate
 figure for railway employees, 91,367, exceeded the Census figure,
 38,049, by 53,318. This is partly explained by the fact that the
 railway headquarters in Bombay report all staff on the sections
 of track for which they have responsibility; areas which extend
 far beyond the city itself. There is also the fact that a substantial
 proportion of those railway employees who work in Bombay
 make use of free travel facilities to reside outside the municipal
 limit. It is assumed that all of the discrepancy is due to the
 Directorate's figure including non-residents, for one of these
 two reasons, which, it is further assumed, account for about
 equal numbers, i.e. that there were as many as 27,000 railway
 employees commuting from outside the city limit. In div. 701,
 'Transport by bus or tram', the Census reports 16,263 workers;
 the Directorate 22,412 Organized employees. The major reason
 for this discrepancy was ascertained to be the inclusion of
 some 4,000 electricity workers, employees of B.E.S.T. (Bombay

Electric Supply and Transport) in this division. This number
has been reclassified under Public Utilities, and the remaining
excess of Directorate over Census figures, 2,149, was assumed
to be due to commuters. The total number of non-resident transport employees thus identified was 55,467 (of whom about
2,900 were commuters) and the initial Organized sector estimate was reduce accordingly.

Division 81 Public Administration. In this instance the reported Organized sector figure, 67,201, understated the size of Organized
Employment. The Census figure of 81,882 could not, by definition, include any Unorganized workers, but it did include
some military personnel who were not covered by the Directorate. The difference between the two figures is military employment (not classified under other industries by the Census) minus
any non-residents there may have been in the Directorate figure
for civilian administrators, plus any error in the Organized
figures. In accepting the Census figure as the correct estimate
of Organized employees, we are including some military personnel, excluding any civilian commuters there might have
been, and ignoring any other error in the Directorate figure.
Division 9   Unclassified Employees listed in the Census were arbitrarily assumed to be equally divided between Organized and
Unorganized establishments.

(c) *Factory Act Figures*

The economic meaning of the 'Organized' sector depends upon
the extent of protective legislation and government regulation of
conditions of employment and wages. The Factory Act extends to
all factories employing more than 10 persons and using power, or
more than 20 without power. There were thus employees in factories
employing 10-25 persons with power, and 20-25 without power,
which fell within the scope of legislative protection but outside the
scope of the Directorate figures we have used. If it had been possible
to estimate the number of such people, we could have included them
in our estimate of the Organized sector, but this turned out to be
very difficult so they have been ignored. We have argued that this
omission is not very serious since it is likely that wages will tend
to be somewhat lower and the enforcement of legislation somewhat
weaker in these marginal establishments.

It proved impossible to estimate the extra manufacturing employees in small establishments because (i) detailed Factory Act data were not available for 1961, (ii) for 1966, on which Factory Act data were available, it was very difficult to make a comparison with Directorate data. Apart from covering more establishments, the Factory Inspectorate uses a different form of industrial classification, includes some activities other than manufacturing, reports average daily employment for the year (rather than labour on the rolls on a single day), and excludes some administrative and sales personnel who are counted by the Directorate. On the whole, one can say that factors other than difference in establishment coverage would tend to lead the Directorate to report more employees than the Factory Act. Hence, if for any one industry the Factory Act reports larger employment than the Directorate, this indicates the presence of smaller establishments; but it would not necessarily be surprising to find, as we did, that in other industries the Directorate figure exceeds the Factory Act figure. Comparison of aggregates can be rather misleading. From the attempt at industry-wise comparison for 1966 we could conclude only that the number of employees in small-scale factories lay between 2 and 14 per cent of employment in Organized sector manufacturing. The 1961 Factory Act total for average daily employment in factories, 505,000, probably includes at least 5,000 employees in non-manufacturing activities like electricity generation and laundries. (There were 8,000 of these in 1966.) The remaining excess over our Organized sector figure of 467,000, i.e. 34,000, can be taken as the lower limit of the number of employees in small enterprises. If, following our 1966 exercise, we take 14 per cent of Organized manufacturing as the upper limit, the result is that employment in Factory Act factories outside our figures was probably no more than 70,000. Of the total 122,000 Unorganized employees in manufacturing that we have estimated, somewhere between 34,000 and 70,000 were nominally covered by the Factory Act.

This range can be confirmed and narrowed by comparing the numbers of establishments reported by the Chief Inspector of Factories and by the Directorate for Bombay in 1961. The former figure, 3,886, exceeded the latter, 1,404, by 2,482. This provides an estimate for the number of registered factories excluded from the 'Organized sector', most of which would employ between 10 and 25 persons. As the average employment of these firms must fall between these numbers, the total number of workers involved must lie in the range 24,820 – 62,050 and is likely to be well inside the extremes, somewhere in the region of 50,000.

APPENDIX III.2

Open Unemployment

For reasons discussed elsewhere in the book, we do not think that the number of openly unemployed discloses the true dimensions of the employment problem. Nevertheless, the statistic has its importance at least in political terms. One approach to measuring the number of openly unemployed is to survey the whole population or a random sample of it. The object is to identify those people who were 'out of work' and 'seeking work' during some reference period by means of a questionnaire. The Census uses a reference period of 15 days and the N.S.S. one of 7 days. Such information is limited by the requirement that 'unemployment' be continuous during these arbitrary reference periods and needs careful interpretation if there is marked seasonality in economic activities. Seasonality is probably less important in urban than in rural areas. Other difficulties are connected with how the questions are understood by the respondents. 'Unpaid family workers' may not think of themselves as being 'out of work', nor may they be 'seeking work' if they understand by that working outside the family enterprise. Again, this problem is less important (though it is not absent) in urban areas where the proportion of wage-employees in the labour force is high. For what it is worth, the 1961 Census recorded 80,416 unemployed in Bombay of whom 14,208 were educated to secondary level or above. The 1971 Census did not seek information on open unemployment. This was a regrettable omission because at least as far as the educated are concerned, the concept is a perfectly meaningful one.

An alternative approach to the documentation of open unemployment is to use a somewhat cheaper method of reporting, making use of the institution of the employment exchange where individuals who are seeking work identify themselves by placing themselves on the register. The defects of this source of information are that at any one time not all persons who are out of work but seeking work may register and some people may register who already have jobs but want to change them. Furthermore, job-seekers may register at more than one exchange. If the object is to measure unemployment in a particular locality, another difficulty is that some registrants may not be residents of the locality. Comparison of the Bombay Employment

Exchange figures for job-seekers in 1961 with the Census figures for unemployment bears out these points. The Census reported 80,416 persons as unemployed; the Live Register (admittedly 10 months later)reported 44,037 job-seekers. Evidently, many people who were out of work did not register. On the other hand, the number of educated job-seekers according to the Census was 14,208 and according to the Live Register, 18,412. This suggests that some of those registrants were either employed or not resident in Bombay. If one wants to measure rates of change in unemployment, Live Register figures can be used only on the assumption that the degree of error introduced by the various factors mentioned remains constant. The assumption is a dubious one.

However, in the absence of any better information, we have attempted to draw some inferences about the evolution of open unemployment over the decade from comparisons of Live Register figures with data for Organized employment. Both these are summarized in Table III.9. Between December 1961 and December 1971 the actual number on the Live Register more than doubled (from 44,000 to 90,000) while Organized employment in March 1971 was only 26 per cent above the figure for March 1961. We calculated annual trend rates of increase which for the Live Register figure was 5.6 per cent as against 2.1 per cent for Organized employment; however, the fluctuations in the Live Register figures were also greater. Inspection of the two series reveals a rough inverse relationship between changes in Organized employment and changes in the Live Register over most of the decade. Though there are difficulties of interpretation, the main feature of developments during the decade is clearly the recession in the demand for labour following a peak in the level of employment some time around 1966 which was not surpassed until 1970. The Live Register shows a reverse movement during this period. As the employment series was approaching its peak, the numbers on the Live Register were falling; while employment was falling and stagnating the Live Register was increasing. At the beginning of the decade too the figures are compatible with the hypothesis; the biggest increase in the Live Register was during 1963 when the growth of employment was weak. However, the end of the decade is rather puzzling. The growth of the Live Register during the recovery of 1969-70 was slow as one would expect; but during 1970-71, though employment growth fell only slightly, the Live Register grew very rapidly indeed.

Thus, over most of the decade, the evidence points to the conclusion that rapid organized employment growth does ease the
employment situation. It has been argued by some writers that
the increase in the labour force 'called forth' by increases in organized employment could be large enough to actually *increase* unemployment. But this does not appear to have been the case over
much of the decade. The last year of the decade might, however,
provide a contrary example whose importance is difficult to assess
because of the scanty data. We do not ourselves think it at all probable that the increase in the Live Register during this year can be
attributed to an influx of migrants attracted into Bombay by the economic recovery. Evidence discussed in Chapter II suggests that the
gross rate of in-migration at the end of the 60's was very low in relation to the city's earlier experience. The sharp increase in employment after the recession could however have resulted in an increase in the propensity to register on the part of people already in
the city.

Can we conclude from the faster increase of the Live Register
compared to the labour force between 1961-71 that the rate of unemployment also increased over this period? Not necessarily, because the propensity to register undoubtedly increased. Evidence
on Bombay from the National Sample Surveys conducted in the
mid-60's show unemployment rates about one half that in the 1961
Census.[15] This suggests, given the increase in the labour force of
about 33 per cent over the decade, that the absolute numbers openly
unemployed must have dropped between 1961 and 1966. However,
during this period, registrations increased by 14 per cent which
must clearly be the result of an increased propensity to register.
After 1966, open unemployment almost certainly rose, absolutely as
well as proportionately, but this need not have been the sole cause
of the rise in the Live Register. By 1971, the unemployment rate may
have reached or surpassed the 1961 level but one cannot know for
certain, indeed one will never know since the 1971 Census did not
ask the relevant questions.

Table III.9

Organized Employment, Registered Job Seekers and Unemployment, Bombay, 1961-71

	1961	1962	1963	1964	1965	1966	1967	1968	1969	1970	1971
Organized Sector Employment '000	883°	908	941	657	1009	1046	1041	1036	1039	1078	1111
Registered Job Seekers '000											
Total	44.0	45.1	56.8	60.2	55.5	50.2	55.5	60.9	61.1*	70.2	90.7
Educated	18.4	17.1	19.1	19.7	19.7	n.a.	24.9	25.2	26.5	29.6	43.5
Surveyed Unemployed	Census*				NSS 20th Round July 65 to June 66	NSS 21st Round July 66 to June 67					
'000 Total	80.4										
Educated	14.2										
Unemployed as percentage of Labour Force	4.55				2.32	1.64					

*March

*September

DEFINITIONS

Organized Sector: Public Sector and Private Sector Establishments employing more than 25 persons. Figures for March (unless otherwise stated). No attempt has been made to exclude non-residents of Bombay.

Registered Job Seekers: Number on the Live Register of the Bombay Employment Exchange at the end of December.

Educated: Educated to secondary level or above.

Unemployed: Seeking work but out of work for the 15 days (Census) or 7 days (NSS) prior to enumeration.

SOURCES

Organized Sector: Directorate of Employment, Government of Maharashtra, Bombay, Quarterly and Annual Returns for 1963-5, 1967-71; and *The Bombay Market* (1966), for 1961, 1962 and 1966.

Live Register: Directorate of Employment, Government of Maharashtra, Bombay; *State Employment Review*, 1968-71 and *The Bombay Labour Market*.

NSS (National Sample Survey), 20th Round—unpublished results of State level sample, by courtesy of the Director, Bureau of Economics and Statistics, Bombay; approximately 1 in 100 households; 21st Round—published Report No. 131, Table (1.2); sample in Bombay City of 24,950 persons, approximately 1 in 200 households.

APPENDIX III.3

The Working Population according to two Censuses and Organized Sector Employment, Greater Bombay, 1961 and 1971

	Population	Workers	Cultivators and Agricultural Labourers	Livestock, Forestry, Fishing, Mining, etc.	Household Manufacturing	Non-Household Manufacturing	Construction	Trade & Commerce	Transport & Communication	Public Utilities & Other Services
1961										
MALES										
Census	2,496,176	1,540,861	4,100	22,316	16,435	632,130	40,223	286,669	180,315	358,673
Organized	—	784,302	—	541	—	444,099	26,787	53,309	97,615	161,951
FEMALES										
Census	1,655,880	145,807	2,689	2,815	6,607	33,400	4,683	17,148	8,943	69,520
Organized	—	53,248	—	20	—	22,552	1,761	2,737	3,585	22,593
PERSONS										
Census	4,152,056	1,686,668	6,789	25,131	23,042	665,530	44,906	303,817	189,260	428,193
Organized	—	837,550	—	561	—	466,651	28,548	56,046	101,200	184,544
1971										
MALES										
Census	3,478,378	2,005,728	4,685	20,167	24,853	855,699	61,181	464,902	226,654	347,587
Organized	—	1,007,015	—	397	—	547,262	27,599	70,310	131,415	230,032

FEMALES									
Census	2,496,176	192,3/0	945	1,865	4,289	44,662	5,831	26,613	10,245	97,920
Organized	—	83,846	—	26	—	23,302	1,333	7,962	5,106	46,117
PERSONS									
Census	5,970,575	2,198,098	5,630	22,032	29,142	900,361	67,012	491,515	236,899	445,507
Organized	—	1,090,861	—	423	—	570,504	28,932	78,272	136,521	276,149

SOURCES:

Census of India 1961, vol. X Maharashtra, pt. X (1-B); *1971*, Series II—Maharashtra, pt. II-A, General Population Tables; Directorate of Employment, Bombay, Quarterly Returns, 1961 and 1971 and *The Bombay Labour Market*. Adjustments have been made to cover non-reporting establishments and non-comparability with Census due to the inclusion of non-residents of Bombay in Organized employment and its exclusion of military personnel. Most of the adjustments for 1961 are explained in notes to Table III.2; additional adjustments on the basis of rough assumptions have been made as follows:

Construction, 1961: reported male employees exceeded those recorded in the Census. The excess were assumed to have been mis-classified Public Utility workers and included in last column. This procedure may not be justified, as there could be other explanations for the discrepancy.

Trade and Commerce, 1971: deductions to allow for commuters of 1,000 males and 500 females.

Transport and Communications, 1971: deductions to allow for commuters and out-of-town railway employees of 60,000 males and 3,000 females.

Other Services, 1971: addition to male employees of 45,000 to cover military personnel net of commuters; net deduction of 500 from the number of females on the same counts.

Total adjustments to reported Organized figures in 1971: deductions of 16,000 males and 4,000 females.

NOTES

1   See L. K. Deshpande, 'Evolution of the Wage Structure in Bombay City, 1950-60' (Unpublished Doctoral thesis, Bombay University, 1964).

2   See Appendix III.1, part (c).

3   The geographical area considered to constitute the Metropolitan Region for the purposes of the Metropolitan Plan covers those *talukas* of Thana district which are immediately adjacent to Greater Bombay and that part of Kolaba District which lies due east of Bombay islands. Ideally one would have liked to compare figures for the growth of Organized employment and working population of this Metropolitan Region as a whole, but the only figures from beyond Greater Bombay that we managed to obtain referred to Thana district. These will exclude the industrial development in the Kolaba part of the Metropolitan Region and include some parts of Thana district which are not in the Metropolitan Region but the vast majority of Thana's urban population is within the Metropolitan Region and so probably is that of its Organized sector.

4   This figure could well be higher. The labour force in the urban areas of Thana district probably grew as fast as the population, because in contrast to Bombay the proportion of males in the population increased slightly since 1961. In 1961 there were 823 females per thousand males in the urban areas of Thana district; in 1971, the sex ratio had dropped to 812. A falling sex ratio is likely to be associated not only with a rise in the proportion of the population in the labour force because males have a higher participation rate, but because it is also likely to be associated with in-migration of working-aged males and therefore with a shift of the age structure in favour of working-aged groups. We have as yet no direct evidence on these points but it seems that to assume the Thana urban labour force grew at the same rate as the population, 65 per cent, is conservative. If the Thana labour force grew by 65 per cent the combined labour force grew by 38 per cent.

5   See P. M. Visaria, *Report of the Committee of Experts on Unemployment Estimates* (1970), app. V. This rate applies to persons in the labour force aged 15-59, excluding unpaid family workers.

6   A rural-urban breakdown of Organized employment is regrettably not available. A substantial but erratic proportion of reported employment in construction is engaged in rural public works. Many of those reported in these categories from urban areas have very much poorer conditions of employment than those in regular manufacturing or tertiary organized jobs.

7   The Registrar-General's projection of the urban labour force for this period was an annual rate of growth of 3.5 per cent. Note also that the observed inter-censal growth of the population of Urban India was about 3.2 per cent p.a. and there is no strong reason to suppose that the increase of the urban labour force would have been much lower.

8   For calculating industrial distribution of the unreported in 1961, it was assumed that all the unreported employees were in the private sector.

This assumption would bias comparisons of the growth of the two sectors if some of the unreported had been in the public sector. The index numbers given in *The Bombay Labour Market* (*idem*) imply that public sector employment in 1961 was in the region of 330,400, rather than the reported 323,375. We have, therefore, assumed that 7,000 of the unreported 67,000 should be attributed to the public sector, but we have left the industrial distribution unchanged. This should serve as a reminder of the shakiness of our base-year figures and of estimates of change based upon them.

9 The following figures for changes in the average levels of outputs and inputs of the Bombay cotton mills between the last three years of the fifties and the end of the sixties indicate that the ratios of capital and material inputs in relation to labour have increased.

Cotton Mills in Bombay : Index of Inputs and Outputs, 1968-70
1958-60=100

Average Daily Working		Cotton			
Spindles	Looms	Consumption (Bales)	Daily Employment	Yarn (tons)	Cloth (metres)
108	95	96	89	93	84

Source: *Millowners Association Annual Report*, 1971.

The productivity of labour too almost certainly increased. Of course, one cannot be certain of this without information on the value of output. As shown below, the average quality of products improved so that the crude volume measures of yarn and cloth overstate the fall in production, whose value may even have increased. Additional evidence that the quality of output improved is provided by the increase in the ratio of spindles to looms—finer cloth needs a greater length of yarn.

Quantities of Cloth Produced in Bombay Cotton Mills by Grade of Cloth

Quality	Thousand metres		Percentage of total	
	1961	*1970*	*1961*	*1970*
All	1371	1120	100	100
Coarse	241	136	18	12
Medium	990	674	72	60
Fine & Superfine	140	311	10	28

SOURCE: *Indian Textile Bulletin*, 1961 Annual, and Monthly Bulletins 1971.

Without better information on the quality of output or machinery we are unable to say whether the productivity of capital also increased. If it did, then the replacement of labour by capital would not have been a case of pure factor substitution.

10   The calculation was made as follows: between March 1969 and March 1970, public sector employment in banking rose by 15,828 and private sector employment in banking fell by 14,180. The former figure is the upper limit of the numbers that could have changed sectors assuming that, in the absence of nationalization none of the overall increase in banking employment would have occurred in the public sector; and the latter figure is the lower limit of the numbers redistributed, assuming that in the absence of nationalization, the private sector would not have expanded employment at all. Since neither assumption seems warranted, 15,000—almost exactly mid-way between these alternatives—is assumed to represent the extent of sectoral redistribution.

11   Super-abundant staffing of government departments is nothing new—it is part of Indian tradition, not specifically a consequence of the post-Independence population explosion, and one would not therefore expect relative growth rates to reveal it. For an account of bureaucratic personnel and procedure at the end of Sixteenth Century, see W.H. Moreland, *India at the Death of Akbar* (London, 1920), pp. 73 and 74. 'There were large clerical establishments at various administrative headquarters....The employment of a large staff of clerks can be inferred from the course of official procedure which was extremely complicated and involved the use of many registers, features which still distinguish the practice of Indian public offices....Travellers give us glimpses of elaborate formalities implying a fully organized administration and we may conclude that in Akbar's time, as at the present day, clerical service afforded employment to a substantial proportion of the population of the country.'

12   Detailed figures are given in Appendix III.3 which shows figures for males and females separately. Even though changed census procedures are likely to have had a greater impact on the numbers of female workers reported, the main pattern of changes shown in Table III.8 is the same when male workers are considered separately.

13   *Mass Transportation Study of Greater Bombay* (Bombay, 1969).

14   *The Bombay Labour Market* (Directorate of Employment & Training, Bombay, 1966).

15   This is despite the more catholic definition of unemployment used by the N.S.S. which involves a shorter reference period: one need only be seeking and without work for 7 days instead of 15 to qualify as 'unemployed'. One has to make several reservations about this comparison. Firstly, figures relating to a particular date (such as the Census and indeed the Live Register) could reflect seasonal factors which should not affect information gathered over a twelve-month period. Secondly, one must express reservations about the reliability of the figures from the samples. In the first place there is the possibility of sampling error, and in the second, more seriously, the sampling frame, based upon households, excludes the houseless part of the population. The latter, the 'pavement dwellers', probably have atypical labour-force participation and could well include a higher proportion of the unemployed than the population at large. However, if the total number of houseless persons

that the 1961 Census managed to record (62,000, equivalent of 4 per cent of the labour force) is any guide to the order of magnitude of the houseless population in the middle of the decade, it seems extremely unlikely that the inclusion of unhoused unemployed persons would raise the mid-decade unemployment rates to anything near the level reported by the Census.

CHAPTER FOUR

THE STRUCTURE OF INCOMES

In Bombay, as in the rest of the country, a very substantial section of the working people live in conditions of poverty. But it is a striking fact that though most incomes in the organized sector are very low, they are, in general, considerably higher than those in the unorganized sector. In this chapter we attempt, in a rough and ready manner, to describe quantitatively the extent of the difference in earnings and in levels of living. This is a matter of some significance for two reasons:

(*a*) Since earnings provide some indication of labour productivity at the margin, the earnings differential between the two sectors suggests a possible misallocation of resources.

(*b*) The inter-sectoral earnings differential throws some light on the sources of economic inequality in the city and in the country generally.

We begin by presenting information on earnings differentials between Organized and Unorganized *unskilled employees*. We then proceed to discuss income distribution in the city more generally.

A. THE EARNINGS OF UNSKILLED EMPLOYEES IN THE ORGANIZED AND UNORGANIZED SECTORS

To avoid confusion, we begin with a brief note on the terminology to be followed in this chapter. The monthly *pay* of a time-rated worker in organized industry consists of three elements: (a) the basic wage (b) the dearness allowance which is supposed to neutralize, fully or partly, changes in the cost of living (D.A.) and (c) bonus and other allowances. We have used the term *wages* to mean (basic wages+D.A.) and the term *pay* to mean (basic wages+D.A.+ bonus). The term *earnings* is used to refer to what the worker actually receives which may be greater than pay because of overtime, piece-rates etc. In the unorganized sector, actual earnings may be less than pay: in this case, monthly or hourly wage-rates may give no indication of actual earnings because of the irregularity of employment. The *take home pay* of a worker in organized industry would be less than his earnings because of statutory Provident Fund contributions and because of income-tax deducted at source. The latter consideration, however, does not affect any of the unskilled workers. As far as unskilled employees are concerned, what one really wants to know about is comparative earnings but the information is hard to come by. We have to make do with data on wages or pay in the Organized sector and information on legislated minimum wage rates in the Unorganized sector.

The data on comparative earnings of unskilled employees in Bombay is presented in Table IV.I with January 1968 as the date of comparison. In the case of the Organized sector the data refer to the monthly pay (and in some cases wages) of the least skilled workers: what an unskilled worker who has gained a regular appointment and not earned any increment or promotion could expect to earn. Peons, sweepers and general labourers would be found at this bottom end of the scale. The information on earnings in the Unorganized sector is much less satisfactory. It consists of the monthly earnings of unskilled workers outside the Organized sector *on the assumption* that they find work for 26 days at the average daily wage. The details about each item are to be found in the Appendix at the end of the chapter.

Despite the very patchy information available, it is clear that earnings in the Unorganized sector are considerably below those in the Organized sector. Table IV.1 probably overstates Unorganized earnings (though to what extent it is difficult to say) because full-time regular work may not be readily available. On the other hand, for several reasons given below, Table IV.I probably understates Organized earnings and the extent to which Organized workers are better off compared to their Unorganized counterparts.

(*a*) Some of the information on Organized earnings listed in Table IV.I relates to wages rather than pay because details about bonus paid were not available. We do know, however, that the Bonus Act of 1965 requires all establishments employing more than 20 workers to pay bonus, the minimum being 4 per cent and the maximum being 20 per cent of wages. Further, there are reasons to believe that we have understated Organized

Table IV.1

Lowest Pay of Unskilled Labour in Various Occupations, Bombay, January 1968

Rupees per month	Organized Sector	Unorganized Sector	Rupees per day
60-69		Women in construction (h); unskilled workers in small hotels (1)(b).	2.30-2.70
70-79		Light work in rice, flour and *dal* mills (2) (b), in road construction (3)(b) and in stone-breaking and crushing (4) (b); some types of work in the *bidi* industry (5)(b).	2.70-3.00
80-89		Glass industry (6)(b); plastic industry (7)(b); oil mills (8)(b); potteries (9)(b); tanneries and leather (10)(b); rubber (11)(b); heavy work in rice, flour and *dal* mills (12)(b) and in stone-breaking and crushing (13)(b); fishermen (14) (c); unorganized coolies in docks (15)(d); unorganized soap production (h).	3.00-3.50
90-99		Heavy work in road construction (16)(b); paper board (17)(b); shops and commercial establishments (18)(b); public motor transport (19)(b); bricks and roof tiles (20)(b); small hospitals (a); small engineering firms (21)(a); male construction labour (h).	3.50-3.90
100-109		Cine studios and cine laboratories (22)(b); canteens and clubs (23)(b).	3.90-4.25

Wage		
110-119		*Bidi* rollers (24)(b).	4.25-4.60
120-129		Average wages of Rs 127.85 in 14 engineering firms employing less than 25 workers (a); printing (25)(b); cinema exhibition (26)(b); auto workshops and garages (27)(b); cotton ginning (28)(b).	4.60-5.00
130-139	Average wages of Rs 139.40 in 18 engineering firms employing 25-49 workers (a); Two chemical firms employing 40 workers each (a); film industry (29)(a).	Railway porters (h); several small-scale manufacturing firms (h).	5.00-5.40
140-149	Jai Hind Oil Mills (a).		
150-159	Pay of the lowest grade of workers in Central and State Secretariats, post offices, railways, other Central and State Government Offices and Administrative Units; Bombay Municipal Corporation (30) (h); average wages of Rs 155.35 in 12 engineering firms employing 50-59 workers (a); some firms producing rubber products (a) and pharmaceutical products (a); recommended wages for electrical undertakings (d).	Metal porters (31)(c); *mathadis* (32)(c); private bargemen in port (33)(d).	5.40-5.80 / 5.80-6.10
160-169	Airlines (e).		

Table IV.1 (Cont.)

Rupees per month	Organized Sector	Unorganized Sector	Rupees per day
170-179	Average wages of Rs 171.49 in 10 engineering firms employing between 100-199 workers (a); Organized port employees (d); recommended minimum wages in heavy chemicals and fertilizers (d).		
180-189	Average wages of Rs 186.20 in 9 engineering firms employing between 200-299 workers (a); Indian Trade and General Insurance Co. (f); silk textile workers (24).		
190-199	Semi-decasualized stevedores (d); recommended minimum wages in cement firms (d); Class 'C' banks (f); Life Insurance Corporation of India (f).		
200-209	National Organic Chemicals Industries (35)(h).		7.70-8.00
210-219	Class 'B' banks (f).		
220-229	Cotton mills (36)(g); decasualized dock workers (d); petroleum marketing (e); Class 'A' banks (f); average wages of Rs 225.76 in 12 engineering firms employing more than 300 workers (a); National Machinery Manufacturers Ltd. (h); Garment Cleaning Works (a); Bombay Electric Supply and Transport Undertaking (h).		
230-239	Tata Oil Mills (a); Associated Cement Company (f).		

240–249	Oil Refineries: Esso, Burmah-Shell (37)(e); Reserve Bank of India (f); Bharat Bijlee Ltd. (h); Voltas Ltd. (h); Poysha Ltd. (h).	
250–259	Mukand Iron and Steel Works Ltd. (h).	
260–269	Phillips (India) Ltd. (h); Paper Products (h); Metal Box Ltd. (h); Indian Aluminium Co. Ltd. (h); Guest, Keen and Williams Ltd. (h).	10.00
270–279	Chemicals & Fibres of India Ltd. (h).	
280–289	Crompton, Greaves Ltd. (h); Sandoz (India) Ltd. (h).	
Above 290	Siemens India Ltd.: Rs 310.63 (h); New India Assurance Co. Ltd.: Rs 315.50 (f); Hindustan Lever Ltd.: Rs 325.4 (f); Cynamid Ltd.: Rs 346.15 (f); Pfizer (India) Ltd.: Rs 366.00 (f); Glaxo Laboratories (India) Ltd.: Rs 393.60 (f).	

NOTE: The numbers in brackets refer to notes on each item and the letters in brackets refer to the sources of the data. Both these are to be found in the Appendix at the end of this chapter.

wages to some extent for reasons explained in the Appendix.

(b) We have not taken account of various fringe benefits which Organized workers receive. Some of them are explicit subsidies. For example, the firm may pay for workers' uniforms. It may allow workers to buy company products at cheaper than market prices. It may run a free medical unit and surgery. It may provide subsidized food during working hours. There are also many allowances specific to occupation and location (32 of them have been listed by the Norms Committee) which are known to contain hidden subsidies, e.g. transport allowance, city allowance, house-rent allowance, machine allowance, cash-handling allowance etc. Some businessmen we talked to estimated that such fringe benefits could be given a monetary value amounting to 7-8 per cent of wages.

(c) Several firms pay favourable rates for overtime work and some have incentive-schemes based on productivity norms. These may add substantially to the earnings of some Organized workers.

(d) Most Organized workers are covered by Provident Fund Schemes to which both employers and employees contribute 8 per cent of monthly wages. The figures given in Table IV.I exclude the employers' contributions.

(e) Many firms in the Organized sector give gratuities on retirement.

(f) In most Organized firms there is a statutory medical and accident insurance scheme to which the employers in 1968 contributed 3 per cent of monthly wages. (This has now been raised to 4 per cent of monthly wages).

(g) Workers in most Organized firms are entitled to at least a month's paid leave every year (taking 'privilege' and 'casual' leave together) and, in addition, more leave in the event of ill-health.

(h) There are other benefits from Organized employment which cannot easily be given a monetary value but which are nevertheless significant and substantial. There is the stability of employment, the security of tenure, certain minimum standards for the physical conditions of work, on all of which the worker is protected by the Factory Acts and other detailed industrial legislation. Further, trade unions in the larger firms are, on the whole, much better organized and much more effective than in the smaller firms and better able to protect workers' interests.

(*i*) Table IV.1 gives some indication of the earnings differentials for unskilled workers. It should be remembered, however, that most workers in the Organized sector earn more than the amounts shown because the starting pay of unskilled workers forms only *the floor* of a wage structure. Not only do skilled workers get more but in many Organized firms, even an unskilled worker's pay would increase with length of service in the firm. On the other hand, in the Unorganized sector where differences in pay as a result of skill and of length of stay tend to be smaller, our figures which specifically relate to the least skilled and lowest paid will in fact be fairly close to the earnings of a 'representative worker'.

There is of course a continuum of earnings within each of the two sectors, as revealed by Table IV.1. The lowest earnings of any activity which we have recorded were being paid to workers in small hotels, i.e. Rs 65 p.m. which includes an allowance for their free food. These workers are largely newly arrived young male migrants who are without dependants and who also sleep on the premises; indeed, on such low incomes they would not be able to support or house any dependants. It must be recorded here that we have no positive proof that the activities recorded as Unorganized in Table IV.1 consisted entirely of establishments employing less than 25 people. This need not be the case, for example, of casual labour in construction. But we are sure that the wage data do refer to activities which *should* be classified as unorganized except for the *mathadis* on whom we comment below. As we have already explained in the previous chapter, our statistical criterion for demarcating the organized sector is, in general, too strict. The wage differentials between the various Unorganized firms in Table IV.1 should not be taken too seriously since much of the information refers to minimum wages fixed at different dates (between 1965-70). The legislated minimum wages are not a bad indicator of the prevailing average level of actual daily earnings. The enforcement machinery for the Minimum Wage Act is extremely weak and there are no doubt cases of actual daily wages being below the legislated minimum. At the same time, it is clear from the minimum wage reports that there has been no attempt by the Committees consciously to raise minimum wages beyond the 'capacity to pay' of the employers concerned. Our impression is that minimum wages are not effective as minima but are representative of the *average* level of *daily* earnings. We do not, however, have any information on the number of days in a month that workers in the various activities are typically likely to find work. We have assumed that it is 26 days in a month but that is undoubtedly an overestimate. The *mathadis* (headload carriers) and the metal porters are the highest paid Unorganized workers shown in the Table. This needs some comment. They are Unorganized according to our statistical criterion since they are technically self-employed, working on a casual or contract basis. In fact, they have an effective union. By wage-bargaining and maintaining a closed shop they have succeeded in creating a situation in which most of them earn more than Rs 160 p.m. (even allowing for the irregularity of work availability).

There is also considerable variation in earnings within the Organized sector. The highest earnings (more than Rs 350 p.m.) were those of workers in the partly foreign-owned pharmaceutical firms who consciously operate a high-wage policy in order to ensure a high-quality and committed labour force and also as a defence against accusations of profiteering. Earnings in the cotton textile industry are also quite high for historical reasons. It has been argued that in the formative years of the Bombay cotton industry, the Mill-owners used high wages as a means of selecting, out of a potentially large pool of labour, a group who had some experience in the industry. Whatever the validity of this analysis, it is true that wages paid in the cotton mills started off relatively high in spite of the abundance of labour. There has also been a long tradition of trade-union activity in the industry so that wages have remained high though it is now a declining industry. Cotton-mill wages are a benchmark for wages in Bombay. The textile Dearness Allowance (which provides 97 per cent neutralization of cost-of-living changes for unskilled workers) is paid by many other enterprises and wages at the upper (but not the extreme) end of the range of Organized sector wages clustered round the cotton-mill level of Rs 225 p.m. in January 1968. Public sector employment was on a broad band around Rs 160 p.m. The entire spectrum of unskilled wages in the Organized sector was very wide—ranging from Rs 130 p.m. to Rs 390 p.m.

We have tried to obtain some information concerning the relationship of wages to employment-size of firm in the private sector. The wage data were calculated from information about agreements and awards contained in the reports of the Norms Committee, Government of Maharashtra. As explained in the notes on sources of Table IV.1, only a small part of the information from the Norms Committee Report could be considered reliable and complete. The only industry for which anything like a complete coverage was possible was engineering in which there was full information on 75 firms of different employment-sizes, based on awards decreed between 1963 and 1968. In this sample of firms at any rate, the expected relationship between wage rate and employment size was seen to hold as Table IV.2 shows.[1] The employment data were obtained from the Factory List maintained by the Commissioner of Labour.

The available information was too incomplete to give anything like inter-industry wage differentials in the Organized sector. But such information as was available in the Norms Committee Report distinctly supported the hypothesis that wages were relatively lower in the older more labour-intensive industries—paper, printing, hotels, cinema production and exhibition, glass, wood, cotton-ginning, leather and tanneries—and that they were relatively

Table IV.2

Unskilled Monthly Wages, Engineering Industry, Bombay, January 1968

Size of Employment	No. of Firms	Average Monthly Wages (Rs)
0—24	14	127.85
25—49	18	139.34
50—99	12	155.35
100—199	10	171.49
200—299	9	186.20
300+	12	225.76

SOURCES: The wage figures have been worked out from information on awards and agreements contained in the *Report of the Norms Committee*, Government of Maharashtra, 1969. See the note on Table IV.1. in appendix IV.1 at the end of the chapter for further elaboration on the method of calculation. The data on employment-size for the relevant firms were obtained from the Factory List maintained by the Commissioner of Labour, Bombay.

higher in the capital-intensive growth industries in Bombay, viz. engineering, chemicals and pharmaceuticals. Cotton mills, of course, paid high wages for historical reasons. It should be noted, however, that even in the industries paying lower wages, typically the two or three large leading firms were always in the high-wage category.

While there is a continuum of earnings in both sectors, our view is that the information regarding relative wages in the Organized and Unorganized sectors can be meaningfully characterized by a representative inter-sectoral 'earnings-differential' for unskilled employees. In the Unorganized sector average pay can be taken to be around Rs 90-Rs 100 per month in January 1968, though actual earnings are probably lower than that due to less than full-time employment. Organized sector wages as presented probably understate the true figures of pay and earnings for reasons already commented on. Roughly 25 per cent of the workers in the Organized sector are employed in cotton-mills in which the unskilled wage was Rs 225 p.m. excluding bonus. Inclusive of bonus, it would vary between Rs 237 and Rs 270 depending on the firm concerned. Thirty-three per cent of the Organized workers are employed in the public sector where the lowest wages are around Rs 160 p.m. As for the rest, there is a dispersion of starting unskilled wages between Rs 130 and Rs 390. However, we can go a bit further. It appears to be the case that 84 per cent of the workers in the private Organized sector in the Bombay-Thana area are employed in establishments employing more than 200 workers. In other words, two-thirds of the non-cotton workers in private manufacturing are employed in establishments employing more than 200 workers.[2] If the relationship between employment-size of firms and wages that we observe for engineering is generally true (and that is our distinct impression from the Norms Committee data) it would appear that the majority of the workers in the private Organized sector are in firms where the pay of the unskilled is between Rs 180 and Rs 250 p.m. Taking all these facts together, we estimate that the earnings differential between the Organized and Unorganized sectors is unlikely to be less than 100 per cent and could easily be as high as 150 per cent. If we also make some allowance for the present value of the employers' provident Fund contributions and for the monetary value of various fringe benefits, we believe that 150 per cent provides the more likely figure.

A further point to be noted is that the *cost to the employer* of hiring a worker is substantially greater than the worker's take-home pay. The employer in the Organized sector had to contribute 11 per cent of wages for Provident Fund and medical insurance together. Further, the month of paid leave to which every worker is entitled is a financial burden to the employer in so far as he has to find a replacement for the worker during his absence. (In fact, encashment of leave is often an option). We present below in Table IV.3 the relevant information concerning the cost of hiring labour in January 1968 in 15 leading Bombay firms. We have taken the employer's Provident Fund and medical insurance contributions to be 11 per cent of the wages. The 'leave salary' is the cost to the employer of replacing the worker while he is on leave on the assumption that he has to pay the same wage to a substitute (or suffer a loss in output equal to that amount). The size of the leave salary has been worked out on the basis of leave provisions in each firm. It can be seen that the financial cost to an employer of hiring unskilled labour exceeds the worker's pay by Rs 50 - Rs 60 p.m. We think these facts point to the conclusion that the private cost of hiring labour is probably about 150 per cent and possibly even as high as 200 per cent above the prevailing wages in the Unorganized sector.

Since 1968, the whole money-wage structure has shifted upward in pursuit of the cost-of-living index. By mid-1971 cotton-mill workers and Government employees were getting about Rs 30 p.m. more than our figures show. Money wages in the Unorganized sector may also have risen, if the upward revision of minimum wages (in those industries where there has been revision) to over Rs 100 has been enforced. There is no reason to believe that our conclusions regarding the Organized/Unorganized earnings differential have been affected.

What are the reasons for this wide disparity in earnings between the Organized and Unorganized sectors? It is too fanciful to suggest that Organized wages need to be so high in order to induce people to give up leisure and not very plausible that the differential is needed to reduce labour turnover and absenteeism, and to make people work under disciplined factory conditions. Employers never complain about the scarcity of labour in general even if they may sometimes complain about the difficulty of finding skilled labour. Another explanation is that labour which is classified as 'unskilled'

Table IV.3

Cost to the employer of hiring the lowest paid unskilled worker in selected leading firms in January 1968

Name of firm	Size of Employment in Bombay area	Monthly Basic Wage+D.A. in Jan. 1968	Bonus	Employer's Provident Fund & ESIC contributions	Leave salary	Total cost to the employer
				Rupees per Month		
1 National Organic Chemicals	442	200	n.a.	22	25	247.00
2 Bharat Bijlee Ltd.	492	218.25	24	24	27	293.25
3 Philips India Ltd.	750	218.25	43	24	25	310.25
4 Paper Products Ltd.	450	233.18	28.51	26	27	314.69
5 Siemens India Ltd.	n.a.	293	17.63	32	44	386.63
6 Mukand Iron & Steel Works Ltd.	539	218.25	33	24	22	297.25
7 Voltas Ltd.	1610	225	18	25	39	307.00
8 Poysha Industries Co. Ltd.	728	224.75	20	25	27	296.75
9 Chemicals and Fibres of India Ltd.	101	225	45	25	33	328.00
10 National Machinery Manufacturers Ltd.	2777	218.55	6.70	24	27	276.25
11 Metal Box Co. of India Ltd.	1652	244.80	24	27	39	334.80
12 Indian Aluminium Co. Ltd.	n.a.	218.77	43	24	22	307.77
13 Crompton, Greaves Ltd.	1163	241.80	40	27	26.5	335.30
14 Guest, Keen Williams Ltd.	674	241.50	20	27	40	328.50
15 Hindustan Lever Ltd.	2677	227.80	45.60	25	27	325.40

NOTE: These firms have their headquarters in Bombay, but may have other establishments elsewhere in the country.
SOURCE: Confidential.

in modern industry is not in fact totally unskilled and that the earnings differential reflects a return to embodied skills and training. We find it difficult to believe this; in many cases the differential is wide though the jobs quite patently do not require any skill (e.g. sweepers and cleaners) or the skill is very easily acquired. A classical explanation for the differential is that employers pay workers more to increase their productivity, i.e. in the interests of profit-maximization. There may well be something in this, though the argument applies equally to Unorganized sector employers. The most important reasons for the earnings differentials between the two sectors would seem to be trade-union activity in the Organized sector combined with, to some extent, the tacit consent of employers. In capital intensive industries particularly, wage costs are a small proportion of value-added which helps to reduce employers' resistance to wage demands. And given that corporation taxes are in the region of 60 per cent, more than half of any wage rise granted is effectively paid for by the Government. An equally important factor, especially with foreign companies, is the desire to maintain good public relations generally and to maintain a contented labour force in particular. In offering higher wages, they can skim the cream of the labour force and appoint to the most menial jobs people to whom they can hold out the prospect of promotion.

Whether or not there are economic explanations for the earnings differentials, the question does arise of the social relevance of a situation where a small minority of often over-qualified people secure a few relatively privileged positions when large numbers are totally excluded. The intellectual climate is also important. Radical and vocal public opinion tends to support Organized industrial workers, ignoring the Unorganized workers in industry and agriculture who are much worse off. The implications of the Organized/Unorganized earnings differentials for employment policy will be discussed in the last chapter.

B. OTHER INCOMES IN THE UNORGANIZED SECTOR

There is some very fragmentary evidence from two sample surveys conducted in the city,[3] which helps to fill out our information on earnings of people working outside the Organized sector. In the mid-fifties when the Lakdawala Economic Survey was carried out, the working class cost of living index for Bombay stood at about half its level in 1968; the regularly employed unskilled worker in textile mills received around Rs 95 per month and the lowest pay in the Organized Sector seems to have been around Rs 75 - 80. Chapter VI of that Survey, dealing with the incomes of earners in sampled households suggests that in certain occupations which we would consider to be entirely Unorganized, earnings were well below this level, around Rs 50 p.m.; there were also a considerable number of occupations which would be outside the large scale sector where average earnings were in the same region as the Organized Sector minimum or even above Rs 100 with instances of earnings above average. These more prosperous Unorganized occupations mostly involved some degree of skill or self-employment. Those with average earnings above Rs 100 included taxi-drivers (Rs 185), *pan-wallahs* (Rs 119), goldsmiths (Rs 108), tailors (Rs 106), barbers (Rs 108), self-employed milkmen (Rs 129), hawkers of textiles and small shopkeepers. The average earnings of predominantly Unorganized occupations such as those of potters, repairers of articles in daily use, newspaper boys and washermen were between Rs 75 and 80, as were those of some workers who would by and large have had large scale employers: peons in the private sector, liftmen and sweepers. The average earnings of unskilled workers in the public sector were higher, between Rs 80 and Rs 90 with very few instances of earners getting less than Rs 75.[4] The relevance of this for our study is that there may be some workers in the Unorganized sector earning as much as the unskilled in the Organized sector. However, closeness of incomes in the two sectors (and the relatively small proportion of earners below the Rs 75 level) which appears in the mid-fifties survey does not constitute strong evidence against our contention that, by the end of the sixties, a large proportion of the incomes generated outside the Organized sector were well below even the lowest pay of regular employees of the Organized sector. In the first place, the sampled population excluded a number of people very probably working outside the Organized sector who are likely to have been among the poorest people as well: houseless persons, living-in domestic servants, lodgers and other families sharing a dwelling with another household. The population so excluded could well be over 20 per cent of the earners.[5] Secondly, there are reasons to believe that the gap between incomes in the Organized and Unorganized sectors has widened since the Lakdawala Survey. These reasons will be discussed in the next section. It is noteworthy that the Lakdawala Survey did not comment upon wage differentials between large-scale and small-scale firms. This survey does, however, contain some interesting information on how the earnings of women were generally below those of men in the same occupational group despite the existence of regulations against discrimination.[6] The ratio of women's to men's earnings was somewhat higher, around 80-90 per cent, in the better regulated and higher-paying occupations than in activities which we would classify as unorganized where it was 50-65 per cent. In the latter case, this is probably the result of two factors—the lack of legislative protection and the greater possibility of working short hours outside Organized employment. It is suggested that the differential observed within the Organized sector is due to fewer women reaching the higher pay scales through seniority or promotion.

The Bulsara Survey conducted in 1963-4 does not give as much detail about the earnings. For the majority of the surveyed population, the data are on the incomes of households rather than of individual earners. Information about earnings for a very small additional sample of pavement dwellers suggests that, at this very low level, the incomes of the self-employed are below those of employees.[7] The average income of 15 self-employed heads of pavement dwelling households was estimated to be Rs 56 per month, that of 21 pavement dwelling employees Rs 85 (or Rs 75 when identifiable employees of the Organized sector are omitted). The lowest regular wage in the Organized sector at this time was around Rs 120.

We conclude that while the Lakdawala Survey creates the presumption that there are some incomes in the Unorganized sector as high as or above the Organized sector minimum, neither sample survey provides any evidence to contradict the hypothesis that there is, in general, a large gap between what can be earned in the two sectors by those with comparably low resources of skill and capital.

C. DISTRIBUTION OF THE INCOME OF EARNERS

In the following two sections we attempt to sketch roughly how the dualistic structure of economic activity affects the structure of incomes and living standards.

Incomes received by the regularly employed unskilled in 1968 were shown above to have ranged from around Rs 60 per month to over Rs 350, the top six times higher than the bottom. This, of

course, can only begin to give an idea of the range of incomes received in the city. Salaries in the public sector ranged up to Rs 4,000
per month and some incomes in the private sector (both salaries and
profit incomes) are even higher. Furthermore, the lowest incomes
are received by those who have no work at all—the unemployed and
the disabled who are forced to beg if their families cannot support
them, but these are excluded from the discussion of the income of
earners.

Table IV.4 shows the results of some rough calculations that can
be made about the distribution of earnings and its relationship to
the structure of the city's economy. The numbers of relatively well-
off income-receivers (arbitrarily defined as those with a *real* income
equivalent to the lowest income which was liable to Income Tax in
1971) were roughly one-fifth of all income-receivers. The proportion
of earners getting less than the lowest incomes obtainable in the
Organized sector was well over one-third—somewhat smaller than
the proportion of workers outside the Organized sector (44 per cent
in 1961) as some earners outside the Organized sector receive incomes comparable to those earned within it. Despite the very rough
basis for these calculations, the apparent rising trend in the proportion of lower incomes is probably significant, since the bias in
the calculations is more likely to underestimate the share of low
incomes in the later years than in the earlier years.

There are other independent reasons to support this hypothesis.
As suggested earlier, it is likely that the gap between earnings of
Organized and Unorganized employees widened during this period.
Prices more than doubled, but only Organized workers were cush-
ioned against cost of living changes by the Dearness Allowance
system. This is not to deny that there are inter-industry and inter-
firm differences within the Organized sector. In the 'growth' industries like engineering and pharmaceuticals, unskilled real wages
probably increased to some extent. In textiles, real wages were
roughly constant. In other declining industries, they may well have
fallen. There were also differences between firms in the same industry, depending on the degree of unionization and on 'capacity to
pay', both of which are roughly positively correlated with employment-size. It should be noted that, in Bombay, the distribution of
the Organized workforce was changing in favour of the skill-intensive industries which were growing and could afford to pay higher
wages. At the same time, the skilled/unskilled occupational differen-

Table IV.4

Estimated Stucture of the Income of Earners in Greater Bombay

	1955-6	1963-4	1971
Percentage of Earners			
Below Organized Sector Minimum	35	37	38
'Middle Class', and above	18	22	18
Current Value of Monthly Earnings (*Rs*)			
Organized Sector Minimum	75	125	200
'Middle Class' Minimum	200	350	500

SOURCES AND NOTES:

1955-6: Lakdawala, *et al.*, op. cit., Table VI-14, amended by the assumption that 20 per cent of all earners were overlooked by the survey of the major households settled in tenements (see note 5) and that the people so excluded earned less than Rs 75. The base should cover *all* earners—full-time and part-time workers and non-working *rentiers*.

1963-4: J.F. Bulsara, op. cit., Tables 144, 149 and 154. In the report on this survey no direct information is given on the income of earners in the surveyed population as a whole but this can be ascertained for the following groups: earners who are heads of single-earner and pavement-dwelling households, and members of migrants' 'chummeries' (households consisting entirely of adult males). This ignores the earnings of earners in other multi-earner households whose inclusion would tend to lower average earnings since the earnings of women and young people tend to be lower than those of household heads and the earnings of household heads in multi-earner households tend to be lower than those of the heads of households where there is no other earner. One can therefore infer that these figures as they stand tend to understate the proportion of earners below the Organized sector line and overstate the proportion in upper income levels.

1971. Information from the Income Tax Commissioner was that in 1971 there were about four and a half lakhs of persons in Bombay assessed for Income Tax—with incomes of at least Rs 500 per month. Two and a half lakhs were salary earners and one and three quarter lakhs had non-salary incomes—*rentiers*, employers and self-employed professionals. If we assume that the total number of earners at the time was 23 lakhs ('full-time' workers reported by the Census 21.9 lakhs, plus allowances for secondary workers and *rentiers*), the income tax assessees were 18 per cent of all income receivers. At this time too there were about 11 lakhs of workers in the Organized sector—8.5 lakhs of whom must have earned between Rs 200 and 500 per month. These would account for another 37 per cent of earners. If no one other than employees of the Organized sector earned as much as Rs 200, there would remain 45 per cent of all income receivers below the Organized sector level. However, we should make some further allowance for people other than Organized sector employees earning between Rs 200 and 500—e.g. the owners of smaller scale businesses and some of the self-employed. If this allowance should be of the order of 7 per cent of all earners, the proportion of incomes below Rs 200 appears to be around 38 per cent.

tials were probably narrowing since D.A. neutralization is much less complete above the unskilled level. As a general statement it is probably quite accurate to say that real wages of Organized unskilled workers in Bombay during the fifties and sixties were roughly constant.[8] On the other hand, the Unorganized workforce was increasing in numbers and possibly as a proportion of the total workforce. It is very likely that without D.A. protection they lost in real terms. Incidentally, this is not incompatible with the national evidence which shows that per capita real consumption of the poorest sections of the urban population fell during this period.[9]

D. INCOME PER HEAD AND POVERTY

To the range of earners' incomes corresponds a range of standards of living. The latter is crudely approximated by the income of a household divided by the total number of people in the household, earners and dependants. People at the bottom of the distribution of per capita income will be members of households where earners are poorly paid, and of households with large numbers of dependants. Low paid earners with no dependants may be as well off as some of the better paid with large families. Household surveys including those done in Bombay (see Table IV.5), show that the population at lower per capita income levels tends on average to belong to slightly larger households. However, the Lakdawala survey also shows that households with high incomes and earners in higher-paying occupations tend to have more dependants. The latter feature is not a mere arithmetical tautology, but suggests that household size and dependancy rates are not independent of income. Factors making for an inverse relationship include (i) higher labour-force participation by women and juveniles in households where adult male earnings are low; (ii) a positive association between the age of the head of the household and both the size of his family and of his earnings; and (iii) two features connected with migration. Migrants with insufficient earnings to support families in the city may be able to leave their dependants at home and bring them in only when their economic position improves; any non-earning newcomers lodging with their kinsfolk are more likely to be found in households which are better able to support them.

Although neither source presents information in such a way as to permit a statistical explanation to be examined, there is evidence in

Table IV. 5

Per Capita Income in Surveyed Households, Bombay 1955-6 and 1963-4

Rupees per capita per month (Current Prices)*	Percentage Distribution of Persons		Persons per Household	
	1955-6	1963-4	1955-6	1963-4
0—15	7.3	6.7	6.9	5.9
15—25	19.5 (26.8)	17.8 (24.5)	6.0	6.2
25—35	21.5*(48.2)	15.0 (39.5)	5.9	5.9
35—50	16.4 (64.7)	17.9*(57.4) ..	4.2	5.2
50—75	14.6 (79.3)	14.8 (72.2)	4.4	4.8
75—100	7.5 (86.8)	8.3 (80.5)	3.8	4.4
100—150	6.7 (93.5)	9.0 (89.5)	3.1	4.4
150—250	3.7 (97.2)	5.9 (95.4)	3.4	3.9
250+	2.8(100.0)	4.6(100.0)	3.7	3.8
Average	Rs 56.8	Rs 70.0	4.7	5.0

NOTES
  Cumulated distribution shown in brackets.
  *Author's 'Poverty Line'.
  *The Bombay working class cost of living index rose by about 35 per cent between the surveys.
SOURCES
1955-6 Lakdawala et al., op. cit., Table V-24.
1963-4 Bulsara, op. cit., Table 134. Samples from Pacca Area and Hutments combined.[10] Insufficient information to incorporate the small sample of pavement dwellers.

the earlier survey that relationships of the first two kinds hold.[11] The explanation related to female participation rates probably would not account for much of the pattern since fewer than 10 per cent, of the families contained women who were secondary earners. There are no suitable tabulations of income, migration status and household composition for the migration-related explanations to be tested. Furthermore, as previously noted, the demographic composition of the sampled population suggests that unaccompanied male migrants are under-represented in the samples. It is in any case especially difficult to make inferences about the standard of living of such people from their incomes. The fact that many workers have no dependants in the city does not necessarily mean that they do not share their earnings at all. They may well have families in their home towns to whom they remit as much of their earnings as they can afford.

Variations in dependancy rates are not large enough to overturn the broad correspondence between per capita incomes and household incomes shown by both surveys, but neither report enables one to compare per capita income with the income of earners. The distributions of per capita household income they reported are shown in Table IV.5. Care should be taken in reading anything into the apparent widening of dispersion in the later survey since the designs of the samples differ, and both under-represent parts of the population.

Each author interpreted such a table by designating an arbitrary level of per capita income as the 'poverty-line'. Lakdawala picked Rs 35 per month, below which nearly half his surveyed population were managing to exist. Writing at a time when the purchasing power of money had fallen, Bulsara designated incomes below Rs 35 as 'destitution'—but found nearly 40 per cent of the population below this level. As a 'poverty-line', he picked Rs 50 which had slightly greater purchasing power in 1963-4 than Rs 35 had at the time of the earlier survey. According to this definition of poverty 57.4 per cent of the surveyed population were living in poverty.

A somewhat more systematic attempt to establish a poverty line was carried out by A. J. Fonseca[12] in an attempt to calculate 'Needs-based minimum wages' for industrial workers in various cities. This took into account the local costs of purchasing a prescribed diet and made certain conventional allowances for non-food expenditure. The requirements of a family of four, a male earner plus wife and two children, in Bombay, were calculated to be Rs 240.88 in 1968. As we have seen, many unskilled workers were getting less than this at that time, even in the Organized sector. Yet this is not such an extravagant definition of poverty—it implies a per capita monthly income of Rs 60 (at 1968 prices). This would have been worth about Rs 38 in 1963-4 or Rs 29 in the mid-fifties—both below the poverty-lines chosen for the two surveys.

Although these poverty-lines are highly artificial, and many people apparently subsist with smaller incomes, they do give some indication of the low level of living standards enjoyed by the majority of the city's population. Most unskilled workers in the Organized sector fall below the 'needs-based minimum' when they have three or more dependants, some unorganized workers as soon as they have to support one or two dependants. Although some un-organized workers, especially younger men and those migrants who can leave their families at home, may have fewer people to support than some Organized sector workers, the distribution of dependants is unlikely to equalize living standards for the majority of unskilled workers in the two sectors. In any case the advantages of the more skilled in the Organized sector remain. As the proportion of mi-grants in the city falls and also as the number of these who have land rights in their native villages falls, the scope for variations in dependancy burdens through migration adjustments will also be reduced. We conclude that while some organized workers live at levels below a 'needs-based minimum', a greater proportion of unorganized workers exist at even lower levels.

Postscript

By the time we finished writing this book, inflation in India had accelerated substantially as a result of bad harvests and the delayed effects of the Indo-Pakistani War of 1971. The wholesale price index increased by 14 per cent between December 1971 and December 1972 and by 26 per cent between December 1972 and December 1973. The prices of many foods increased even faster. The outlook for 1974 is, if anything, worse: on top of internal inflationary tendencies, the world oil price increases are bound to give a further twist to the price spiral.

During these years, organized workers managed, if only barely, to keep pace with the cost of living. In Bombay at the beginning of 1974, Class IV Central Government employees' pay had risen to more than Rs 220 p.m. Cotton textile workers had negotiated a new agreement and their minimum wages had risen to more than Rs 300 p.m. This is exclusive of bonus; the minimum bonus which all enterprises have to pay has now increased to 8.33 per cent of wages, the maximum remaining at 20 per cent. Money wages in organized engineering and pharmaceuticals would appear to have kept pace with prices. In the leading large enterprises in these indus-tries, minimum pay had gone up to between Rs 450-550 p.m.

Inflation does not strike in a fair manner across the board. Orga-nized workers, as a whole, may have suffered some decline in real earnings though particular groups have certainly kept up or even gained. Owner-cultivators (though not necessarily landless labour-ers) in agriculture have, to some extent, been insulated from the effects of inflation. The salaried middle classes were certainly hard hit. But there can be little doubt that the groups which have been hardest hit are the urban unorganized workers. In other words, urban organized/unorganized earning differentials are almost certainly even wider than we had estimated.

APPENDIX IV. I

TABLE IV.1 : SOURCES OF THE DATA

(a) *Report of the Norms Committee*, Government of Maharashtra (1969).

The Norms Committee was appointed by the Government of Maharashtra in 1964 'to examine the Settlements, Agreements and Awards made under the Industrial Disputes Act 1947' from 1959 to 1963 and 'to suggest norms in relation to various industrial matters, including wages and D.A. but excluding bonus' in 27 named industries.

('Agreements' between employers and employees concerning wages, working conditions etc. are binding on both parties but are arrived at without any third-party participation. 'Settlements' are agreements arrived at with the help and participation of a Government conciliation officer. 'Awards' are judicial decisions given by industrial tribunals on reference made to them. Awards and Settlements are automatically registered with the Commissioner of Labour. Most agreements in the Organized sector would be registered with the Commissioner of Labour though this is certainly not the case with the Unorganized Sector).

The Norms Committee submitted its report at the end of 1968. In the meantime it decided (with the consent of Government) to go beyond its initial brief and consider trends after 1963 by examining awards (but not settlements or agreements) from 1964 to the end of 1967. In its Report the Committee did not in fact suggest any norms for basic wages and D.A.; it did, however, make several suggestions for rationalizing various allowances, rules concerning leave and so on.

Along with its main report the Norms Committee published three volumes of information on basic wage and D.A. awards, settlements and agreements from 1959 to 1963 and on awards only from 1963 to 1967. We have tried to use this data in describing the wage structure of Bombay city. We found, however, that the usefulness of the data was severely limited for several reasons. There are two reasons why the Norms Committee would tend to *understate* earnings. The *first* and more obvious reason is that the Norms Committee tells us only about basic wages and D.A. agreements, and gives no information about bonus agreements. *Second*, even on wages, there may be a downward bias. To see this, consider what using the Norms Committee data involves. We took the most recent award or agreement

before our reference date of January 1968 and used its basic wage
and D.A. provisions (if it contained both these) to calculate wages
on our reference date. There is of course a wide variety in the types
of D.A. agreements, but with some care the calculation was feasible.
The difficulty is, however, that the Committee lists only the *awards*
after 1963 and there is no guarantee that these awards (or earlier
awards and settlements) were not superseded by *agreements* or *settlements* after 1963. So we decided to restrict ourselves only to the
awards *after* 1963 to reduce the probability of such a bias. Nevertheless the bias is clearly not completely eliminated. So the Norms
Committee wage data should be taken as being the *lower* limit of
actual wages.

The other problem with the Norms Committee data was its inadequate coverage. Of course, the data is not even remotely like a wage
census. In fact, in most industries there was complete (i.e. covering
both basic wages and D.A.) and recent (i.e. post 1963) information
on only a very few firms. Only in the Engineering Industry was the
sample large enough to draw any conclusions about wages in the
industry as a whole. (These are referred to in the body of the chapter).
In other industries, we had to use the Norms Committee data
cautiously and selectively—either to give a general impression of
prevailing wages in the industry or to pick out known leading firms
when data on them was available.

(b) *Reports of the Minimum Wage Committees of the Maharashtra
    Government.*

The object of the Minimum Wages Act (1948) is to fix minimum wages statutorily in employments where 'sweated labour
is prevalent or there is a big chance of exploitation of labour'.
The Act originally covered 13 employments and the Maharashtra
Government has added another 16.

In fixing minimum wages, the Government appoints a Committee
to hold enquiries and advise it. The reports of the Committees sometimes contain information on the prevailing earnings in the relevant
trade. In such cases, we have made use of the information in Table
IV.1. In other cases, the Committee simply reports the observations
of the employers' and employees' representatives and makes its
minimum wage recommendations which if accepted by the Government (and they almost always are), are published as Government

notifications. In such cases, we have used these minimum wages. The Committees have been very alive to the undesirability of fixing minimum wages which are above 'the capacity of the industry to pay'. Our best guess is that these minimum wages represent *average* unskilled earnings in the trade. Conversations with knowledgeable people suggest that they are not effective as *minimum* wages. This would seem to be plausible in view of the weakness of the enforcement machinery. There is no government staff specifically deputed to enforce the Minimum Wages Act. The Factory Act Inspectors and some other Labour Department officials are expected to perform this function in addition to their other duties. Given the very large number of establishments to be covered, it is impossible to carry out the enforcement.

A few observations about our use of the minimum wage information should be made here. *First*, we have no positive proof that wages as low as minimum wages recorded were being paid only by firms employing less than 25 workers. However, the overwhelming presumption is that this is the case. It is the smaller firms which have no unions or weak unions. The minimum wage reports also contain scattered information on wages in the concerned trades which confirms this relationship between wages and size of employment. *Second*, the recorded minimum wage data do not cover all of the Unorganized sector. There is no information on the earnings of the self-employed and the family workers who account for 40 per cent of the Unorganized sector. Even among employees the minimum wage regulations do not cover a good deal of small-scale manufacturing and personal services. *Third*, the Unorganized employees are covered by some industrial legislation—some of them by the Factory Act, some by the Shops and Establishments Act. But in this range the enforcement of the Acts is negligible.

(c) *Reports of other Committees set up by the Maharashtra Government*

At certain times the Maharashtra Government has appointed committees to consider the problems of certain special groups of workers. We have made use of three such reports: (i) Report of the Lokhandi Jatha Kamgar Enquiry Committee (1965)—*Lokhandi Jatha Kamgar* are metal porters; (ii) Report of the Mathadi Labour Enquiry Committee (1965); (iii) Report of the Committee on Unprotected Labour (1967).

(d) *Reports of Central Wage Boards*

From time to time the Central Government sets up wage boards to determine wages on an industry-wide basis. A wage board is tripartite in character: it consists of an equal number of representatives of employers and workers, an economist, a consumers' representative and an independent chairman. The recommendations of the Wage Boards are non-statutory in character but some effort is made to implement them by the State industrial relations machinery. We have used either observed wage data reported by a wage board or in some cases the minimum wage they have recommended. The four wage board reports which we have referred to are: (i) Wage Board for Port and Dock Workers; (ii) Wage Board for Heavy Chemicals and Fertilizer industries; (iii) 2nd Wage Board for Cement; and (iv) Wage Board for Electricity Undertakings. There have been wage boards for other industries but in these cases, we have obtained more direct information on these industries or they are not relevant for our study of Bombay or we have reason to believe that the wage board recommendations have not been effective.

(e) *Reports of the Study Groups of the National Commission on Labour*

The National Commission on Labour which reported in 1969 studied all aspects of labour questions in India. We have used the reports of two of its study groups—on airlines and on petroleum—to obtain wage information.

(f) *Report of the National Council of Applied Economic Research on the Wage Structure in Indian Banking* (Delhi, 1969).

The principal object of this study was to examine in some detail the evolution of the wage structure in commercial banks. But it also collected valuable information on basic wages, D.A. and bonus in other selected organizations and firms. Since the survey was made in January 1968, the data is exactly comparable with ours. The great virtue of this Report is that it gives us information on *pay*, not just on *wages*.

(g) Millowners' Association, Bombay.

(h) Confidential but reliable sources.

1   The lowest observed wage reported by the relevant Minimum Wage Committee in 1968 was Rs 65 (made up of cash payment of Rs 25 plus food worth Rs 40, assuming that a worker gets all his meals). The Minimum wage fixed in 1966 was Rs 75; in 1969 it was raised to Rs 100. Some agreements reported by the Norms Committee for the hotel industry show wages around Rs 80.

2, 3 & 4   These are minimum wages all fixed in 1965.

5   Minimum wages, fixed for tobacco sorters and some other types of work in the *bidi* industry.

6   This is the lowest observed wage in 1968. The minimum wage was fixed at Rs 80 in 1964 and raised to Rs 108 in 1969.

7   Lowest reported wages in 1968. The minimum wage was fixed in 1969 at Rs 93.60.

8   The minimum wage fixed in 1964 was Rs 80; in 1970 it was raised to Rs 104.

9   The minimum wage fixed in 1964 was Rs 84.50; in 1969 it was raised to Rs 127.40.

10, 11, 12, 13   These are minimum wages fixed in 1964 and 1965.

14   This is the lower range of fishermen's earnings reported by the Committee for Unprotected Labour (1967). The upper range was around Rs 120.

15   These earnings were reported by the Central Wage Board for Ports and Docks (1969).

16 & 17   These are minimum wages established in 1965-6.

18   The minimum wage fixed in 1966 was Rs 90; in 1971 it was raised to Rs 120.

19   The minimum wage fixed in 1964 was Rs 95; in 1971 it was raised to Rs 130.

20   The minimum wage fixed in 1969 was Rs 90.

21   These earnings are worked out on the basis of agreements reported by the Norms Committee. The firms concerned employ less than 10 people.

22   Minimum wages of Rs 100 were fixed in 1969.

23   Minimum wages of Rs 105 were fixed in 1970.

24   These earnings are worked out on the basis of the minimum

piece-rate established in 1968.

25   Printing is one of the few cases in which minimum wage legislation includes some compensation for cost of living increases.
Wages in 1968 taking account of this were about Rs 121 p.m.
Some agreements recorded by the Norms Committee also
mentioned wages around this level.

26, 27, 28.   Minimum wages of Rs 120 in each case were fixed in
1970-71.

29   Three leading film companies(Metro Goldwyn Mayer, Twenti-
eth Century Fox and Warner Brothers paid wages around
Rs 140 according to Norms Committee data. Eleven companies for which complete information exists in the Norms
Committee reports paid an average wage of Rs 130. It is
possible that according to our statistical criterion some of these
companies should be classified as Unorganized.

30.   The new D.A. scheme for municipal employees brought the
lowest pay to Rs 165 from 1.4.1968. The lowest total pay
(inclusive of house rent allowance and city compensatory
allowance) of unskilled Central Government employees was
Rs 157 in January 1968, that of State Government employees
very slightly lower.

31, 32   The relevant report states that the monthly earnings of
metal porters are *at least* Rs 150 p.m. and those of *mathadis
at least* Rs 120 p.m. but many of them earn more—up to Rs
250 p.m. *Mathadis* and metal porters number about 20,000
in all. They are very effectively unionized: an exception among
Unorganized workers.

33   These are earnings reported by the Central Wage Board on
ports and docks.

34   Wages in the silk textile industry are standardized. In 1968
the basic wage was Rs 40, the D.A. was 80 per cent of the
textile D.A. More recently the D.A. has been raised to parity
with the textile D.A.

35   These are wages. Being newly established, the firm was exemp-
ted from paying bonus in 1968.

36   Cotton Mills have standardized wages. Wages for workers in
cotton mills in January 1968 came to Rs 225.75 (basic wages
Rs 40 plus D.A. Rs 185.75). To get total pay we must add
bonus which would vary between 4 and 20 per cent of wages
and of course other fringe benefits, e.g. subsidized housing.

37   These figures are *exclusive* of bonus. Total pay could easily
      be 15 - 20 per cent higher on this count. These oil com-
      panies are also known to give various other allowances in
      substantial amounts.

120   SURPLUS LABOUR AND THE CITY

NOTES

1 The positive relationship between intra-industry employment-size and wages
is presumably to be explained by the fact that the larger firms are more profitable and so can afford to pay higher wages and are under greater pressure
to do so. Industrial tribunals aided this process. They were generally in
favour of the same basic wages throughout an industry but with very
different D.A. and bonus provisions, depending on 'the ability to pay'.
Some scanty data in L. K. Deshpande, 'Evolution of the Wage Structure
in Bombay City, 1950-60 (Bombay University Doctoral Thesis, 1964) tends
to support the hypothesis.

2 See *The Bombay Labour Market*, Directorate of Employment, Govt. of
Maharashtra, Bombay, November 1966.

3 D.T. Lakdawala, *et al., Work, Wages and Well Being in an Indian Metropolis, Economic Survey of Bombay City* (Bombay, 1963)—investigations
carried out in 1955-6 of a 3 per cent random sample of dwellings; and J.F.
Bulsara, *Patterns of Social Life in Metropolitan Areas* (Bombay, 1970), a
sample survey carried out in 1963-4, restricted to selected localities covering about 1 in 300 of the population.

4 Lakdawala, *et al.* op. cit., Table VI-A2, pp. 438 and 528.

5 As noted in Appendix II.1, the survey is likely to have under-represented
certain sections of the population. The ratio of males to females in the sampled population—1159 per thousand—is suspiciously low. In 1951, the sex
ratio was 1,650 and in 1961 it was 1507. If the mid decade sex ratio had been
halfway between these and if the survey had excluded only males, it would
have missed out almost exactly one-sixth of the true population. Since the
excluded population would include some females and very probably a higher
than average proportion of earners, the proportion of *earners* excluded is
likely to be at least 20 per cent. If one makes the same naive assumption
about the number of dependants per earner (2.27 in the survey, 1.15 in the
1951 Census and 1.46 in the 1961 Census) the under-representation of
earners seems more severe—over 40 per cent, but these figures are subject to
additional error because of changes in definitions.

6 See Lakdawala, *et al.*, op. cit., Table VI-31, p. 442.

7 See Bulsara, op. cit., Table 154, p.299.

8 At the all-India level, unskilled real wages in factories would appear to
have fallen somewhat over the period (see the evidence in the *Report of
the National Commission on Labour*, 1969, Table 14.3 and in *Indian Labour
Statistics*, 1970, Table 4.8). It must be remembered, however, that the mid-
fifties are a rather abnormal base for comparison since prices had fallen
in the early fifties and real wages had improved substantially. Furthermore,
the fall in the real wage index may be spurious resulting from(a)the increasing
coverage of workers with low wages and (b) the downward bias imparted
by the exclusion of workers whose money earnings rise with time above
Rs 200 p.m. (with the old index) or Rs 400 p.m. (with the new index). A
useful general reference for national wage developments during the period
is the *Report of the Study Group for Wage Policy* of the National Commis-

sion on Labour, 1969.

9 See V. M. Dandekar and N. Rath, *Poverty in India* (Bombay, 1971), Ch. 2.

10 The accuracy of the overall picture of income distribution given by combining Bulsara's two samples will depend,among other factors,upon whether the ratio between populations living in these two types of housing is accurately reflected in the relative size of the two sub-samples. In fact, the share of hutment dwellers in Bulsara's samples (21 per cent of housed population) is at any rate of the same order of magnitude as their share at the time of the 1961 Census as suggested by tabulations on the material of houses. As the latter do not specifically distinguish hutments it is hard to be precise. The *Report of the Study Group on Housing and Urban Development in Maharashtra* estimated that in 1971 hutment dwellers accounted for about 1,200,000 of Bombay's inhabitants—also around one-fifth of the population. We have not gone any further into questions concerning supply and standard of housing and their relationship to urban growth and living standards.

11 Lakdawala *et al.*, op. cit. Table V-2 shows earner-population ratios against household income, and Tables V-36 and 37 tabulate family income and per capita income respectively against age of head of household. This is tabulated against family size in Table V-35.

12 'The Poverty Line for the Industrial Worker', in A. J. Fonseca (ed), *The Challenge of Poverty in India* (Delhi, 1971).

CHAPTER FIVE

MIGRATION AND THE SUPPLY
OF LABOUR

As the majority of Bombay's population was born outside the city (64 per cent in 1961) and a disproportionate number of them are adult males, Bombay's working population consists overwhelmingly of migrants. In 1961 they accounted for 84 per cent of the working population and 85 per cent of all male workers. Nevertheless these figures, taken at face value, overstate the quantitative importance of the process of migration in adding to the city's labour supply. Firstly, many of the migrant workers have been in the city for a considerable length of time. In 1961, when 84 per cent of the workforce had been born outside the city, only 32 per cent had arrived during the previous decade and only 5 per cent during the previous one year. Secondly, the share of natives in the city's population has been rising over time which makes it likely that their proportionate contribution to the growth of the labour force will increase.[1] Nevertheless, migration remains an important and potentially flexible element in the city's labour supply, more likely than natural population growth to respond to changes in employment conditions. This chapter examines evidence about the sensitivity of this part of the city's labour supply.

An understanding of the migration process is of critical importance in formulating employment policies. The sensitivity of migration to changes in the demand for labour depends partly on the motivations that underlie migration decisions and partly on various characteristics of the mechanisms of recruitment and information dissemination. If the motivation for migration is economic, it may be expected to respond sensitively to changes in job opportunities, with the appropriate allowance being made for costs of moving towards or away from the city. But the extent of the sensitivity depends on other factors as well. For example, it has been asserted by some writers, in the context of Africa, that provision of extra jobs in cities attracts more migrants than the number of jobs offered, thereby adding to the pool of unemployment.[2] As we shall see later, this outcome is compatible with economic rationality on the part of migrants only if the recruitment process has certain specific features. Proper testing of hypotheses about the migration process would require detailed annual data on the size and composition of migration flows as well as on the important explanatory variables, supplemented by fieldwork providing information on the history of migrants of various characteristics coming to the city at various different times. However, Census information is available only every ten years. As for fieldwork, it was not an option open to us and to be done properly would involve longitudinal as well as cross-sectional surveys lasting several years. We have therefore had to restrict ourselves to gathering together and analysing various pieces of information from the Census and from published sample surveys. Imperfect though such a procedure might be, it does lead to some suggestive conclusions.

A. THE MOTIVATIONS OF MIGRATION

All the three sample surveys quoted in Table V.1 report the majority of migrants as giving work-related reasons for migrating. The heading 'economic incentives' in the Table covers people who said they came for better employment opportunities in the city and those who said they came because of economic difficulties at home, such as insufficient land, low income or unemployment. The accounts emphasizing 'push' factors rather than the positive attractions of the city accounted for over three-fourths of the 'economic reasons' in the Lakdawala Survey and about half of the same in the Gore Survey (See below Table V.1). Conceptually, it is difficult to maintain a coherent distinction between 'push' and 'pull' for both sets of accounts imply that the destination is seen as having an economic advantage over the origin. Although those who were 'pushed' out may have had little choice but to leave home, this does not necessarily mean that they had no choice about where to go. Whether the disadvantages of the origin or advantages of the destination are stressed may depend on subjective factors such as the migrants' position *vis-a-vis* others at the origin and their experiences after migration. Few respondents mentioned reasons which would be wholly independent of economic opportunities. Those who accompanied their families may well have been brought along as children when their fathers decided to migrate for work. Those coming for education may also have had the labour market indirectly in mind.

B.   INCOME COMPARISONS AND MIGRATION

One would expect an important factor influencing the decisions of potential migrants to be the difference between income earning opportunities in the city as compared with other places. Income per head in the city was estimated to be three times as great as income per head in the State and in the country.[3] This is not the proper comparison to make in assessing the existence of incentives for migration though it might be of some relevance because the greater overall prosperity of Bombay might give those without specific information about earning opportunities the impression that it presents possibilities for economic advance. The relevant income comparisons clearly vary for different potential migrants and will be affected by (a) variations in the purchasing power of money, (b) variations in dependancy burden and in the stake in family income arising from the move, (c) the relevant difference in earning possibilities between origin and destination given an individual's skill and contacts, (d) prospects for advancement in the different places, (e) the chances of success and failure, and (f) the potential migrant's perception and evaluation of the balance of advantages.

A major difficulty in assessing relative incomes in rural and urban areas is to take account of variations in the purchasing power of money and of other elements of living costs in different places. There have been very few systematic attempts to make spatial comparisons of the cost of living and these do not show cost of living differences to be as large as might be imagined. Table V.2 shows the results of a comparison of rural and urban prices carried out on the basis of household expenditure data from the 18th Round of the National Sample Survey in 1963-4 for India as a whole and for Maharashtra. Price relatives could only be calculated for the items which appeared in the budgets of both urban and rural households and for these the average excess of urban over rural prices was surprisingly low—15 per cent for India as a whole and 8 per cent for Maharashtra. Going further, some allowance must be made for the fact that urban patterns of living require cash expenditure on items

Table V.1

Migrant Workers by Main Reason for Coming to Bombay

Date of Survey	1955-6 % of all mi-grant* earners	1963-4 % of migrant* house-hold heads	Late 60's % migrant workers speaking:		
			Marathi	Hindi	Tamil
Reason for Migration					
Economic Incentives	85.0	65.7	74	82	82
Transfer by Employer	4.2	2.6	5	9	8
Education	3.1	6.8	19	3	3
Accompanied Family	1.8	19.2			
Social tensions of family trouble at home	1.0	1.0	2	5	6
Others and no information	4.7	4.5			
TOTAL	100	100	100	100	100
Number in Sample	(2885)	(2141)	(120)	(120)	(118)

*Refugees from Pakistan not included.
SOURCES:
  1955-6: D.T. Lakdawala *et al.*, op. cit., Table IV.5.
  1963-4: J.F. Bulsara, op. cit., Table 7.
  Late 60's: M.S. Gore, *In-migrants and Neighbourhoods* (Tata Institute of Social Sciences, Bombay, 1970). Date of Survey not specified. The study was confined to adult male migrants speaking each of the three languages and earning less than Rs 500 per month. The sample was further matched to include three manual workers for every two white collar workers. Half the observations are based on a survey of households, half from a survey in two contrasting factories.

such as housing and transport which do not have to be made in the villages. It would be an exaggeration to say that the extra items of expenditure for town-dwellers wholly represent costs which are not incurred by villagers. Some of the services on which town-dwellers spend their money such as entertainment or electricity may not be available in villages. Substitutes for these and items such as housing may be produced at the cost of time and effort outside the monetized sector without being recorded in the expenditure surveys. Excluded items accounted for 14 per cent more of the All India urban budget and 21 per cent more of the Maharashtra urban budget than of their respective rural budgets.

We make a rough and ready allowance for unavoidable costs of urban living assuming that 10 per cent of the All-India urban budget and 15 per cent of the Maharashtra urban budget represent costs which are not incurred by rural dwellers. We then calculate the purchasing power of urban disposable incomes after deducting these costs. This yields a cost of living differential between urban and rural areas somewhat higher than the price index but not staggeringly so, about 28 per cent for both the country as a whole and for Maharashtra.

Table V.2

Rural-Urban Cost of Living Index (1963-4)

Item	All India			Maharashtra		
	Rural Weight %	Urban Weight %	Price Index (Fisher's) Urban ÷ Rural %	Rural Weight %	Urban Weight %	Price Index (Fisher's Urban ÷ Rural %
Cereal } Cereal Substitutes }	40.37	22.55	111.47 }	20.58	29.63	105.47
Other Food	29.71	36.92	113.92 }	50.69	27.26	106.83
All Food	70.08	59.47	112.68	71.26	53.88	106.26
Non-food*	18.11	15.15	126.00	27.56	23.61	113.57
Excluded items	11.80	25.37		1.18	22.50	
TOTAL	100.00	100.00	115.35	100.00	100.00	108.38
Assuming unavoidable urban expenses		10.00	128.16		15.00	127.50
Average per capita expenditure per month	Rupees			Rupees		
	22.32	32.91		21.26	38.90	

*Fuel, clothing and intoxicants. In Maharashtra this item also includes soap and footwear. Housing, transport, ornaments, services etc. are excluded from both indices.

SOURCES All India: G.S. Chatterjee and N. Bhattacharya, 'Rural Urban Differentials in Consumer Prices', *Economic and Political Weekly*, 17 May 1969. Maharashtra: By courtesy of the Director, Bureau of Economics and Statistics, Maharashtra. Both estimates are based upon the N.S.S. 18th Round, Tables on Consumer Expenditure. The Maharashtra price data was collected separately by the Bureau.

Nevertheless, the costs of living in a major city like Bombay are probably higher than in urban areas taken as a whole. Fonseca's calculations of a 'needs-based minimum wage' for various urban centres showed Bombay to have a markedly higher cost of living than other industrial cities, small centres as well as metropolitan areas like Madras and Delhi. The Bombay 'needs-based minimum' was 20 per cent higher than the average for all centres in India and 16 per cent higher than the five centres in Western India which he considered. Again, this is a very shaky base for accurate calculations but one can take it as a rough guideline to say that Bombay costs of living are probably not more than 1.2 times as great as average costs of living in other urban areas, which in turn we have estimated to be not more than 28 per cent above rural costs of living, averaged over households and different parts of the country. This gives a maximum excess of Bombay living costs over rural areas of about 50 per cent.

Armed with an approximate cost of living deflator, we can try to assess the relevant difference in prosperity between Bombay and other parts of the country. We have already argued that income per head figures are unsuitable for this purpose. Evidence somewhat more pertinent than per capita income figures comes from surveys of household income and expenditure. These too give aggregated averages (which however are restricted to incomes received by private individuals) but they also provide details about the distribution behind the aggregates. These are shown in Table V.3. The penultimate row of this table shows the not unexpected result that average expenditure is higher in Bombay than in other urban areas of India, and that it is lowest in rural India. The National Sample Survey also reported a large proportion (about one-quarter) of rural dwellers living at levels below Rs 12 p.m. which did not appear at all in the Bombay sample. Equally striking is the top end of the distribution, where the top half of persons in Bombay had expenditure levels enjoyed by only about 5 per cent of the rural population. The top 30 per cent in rural areas has monthly per capita expenditure of Rs 24 and above; in urban India the top 30 per cent had upwards of Rs 34 but in Bombay this level was probably closer to Rs 75 than to Rs 50. However, these figures make no allowance for differences in the purchasing power of the rupee in different places.

According to the foregoing discussion, an extremely rough adjust-

Table V.3

Levels of Living in Bombay and All India, 1963-4

Rs. per head per month	percentage distribution of sampled persons			
	expenditure			income
	All India		Bombay	
	Rural	Urban		
	(1)	(2)	(3)	(4)
Above 75	1.2	6.1	24.3	27.8
Above 50	3.6	14.6	47.3	42.6
Above 34	12.4	29.8	71.6	60.5
Above 24	30.4	52.1	86.5	75.5
Above 15	68.0	83.6	99.4	93.3
Average (Rs)	22	33	58	70
Number of persons in sample	112,146	19,718	1,030	13,634

SOURCE: Cols. 1, 2 and 3, National Sample Survey, Eighteenth Round, Report No. 142, *Tables with Notes on Consumer Expenditure* (Government of India, 1969), col. 4, calculated from J.D. Bulsara, op. cit.

NOTE: Col. 4 shows greater dispersion than col. 3 with more people in both the top and the bottom ranges. This could be explained by divergences, due to saving or borrowing, between households' income and expenditure. It may also be that at least one of the samples gives a biased result. Both sets of figures exclude the houseless, and Bulsara's sample frame also excluded domestic servants.

ment of the right sort of magnitude would be to shift the figures in the urban columns down one row. There then appear to be a greater proportion of people living at the lowest levels in urban areas than in rural areas despite the higher nominal (and probably real) average in urban areas. This phenomenon was observed by Dandekar and Rath[5] in their analysis of NSS data for other years (1966-7 and 1967-8), but the cost-of-living adjustment would have to be well over our maximum deflator of 1.5 for the same to be true of Bombay.

Higher overall levels in Bombay are not very surprising because of the prosperity of the advanced part of its economy. The interesting question is how far this prosperity percolates down to groups outside the organized sector. For this purpose, one should compare the levels of living in the unorganized sector of Bombay with rural India. This is not so easy. There is no simple way of extracting unorganized workers' families from columns 3 and 4. Organized and unorganized earnings in any case overlap, to a certain extent, and variations in earners per household and dependants per earner mix these two sectors of the population even more when individuals are ranked by per capita household income. The ranking on expenditure would be even further complicated by variations in ratio of income to expenditure. Notwithstanding this, we can make statements to the following effect: the bottom half of the city's population live at levels surpassed by only a very few in rural areas, and the bottom 30 per cent of the population in Bombay has a similar range of expenditure levels as the bottom 70 per cent of the rural population.

The likelihood of an advantage in Bombay also appears if we make the more direct comparison between wage labour in the unorganized sector of Bombay and in rural India. There are separate tabulations of the 18th round of the NSS showing the income of rural households dependent upon wage labour, which are summarized below:

Average Income of Rural Labour Households, All India, 1963-4

| | Rupees per month | | |
	per house-hold	per earner	per capita
Agricultural labour	55.0	27.3	12.3
Non-agricultural labour	71.1	35.7	15.1
All rural labour	55.7	27.9	12.4

SOURCES: NSS 18th Round, Report No. 132; *Tables with Notes on Income of Rural Labour Households*, Government of India, 1969.

It is our impression that earnings in the unorganized sector in Bombay at this time were mostly in the range Rs 50-75 per month, when average rural labour earnings were Rs 28. It should be noted that the rural income per earner figures are pulled down by the inclusion of more lower paid women and juveniles among earners than in Bombay. Nevertheless it would need to be a fairly heavy cost-of-living deflation of urban rupees—dividing by at least 1.5, which is probably too generous—to bring the lowest Bombay earnings right down to rural levels. To what extent there are households in Bombay living at the per capita income level of average rural landless labour depends likewise on how much allowance should be made for cost-of-living adjustments, as well as which source of information is used. The NSS Expenditure figures in Table V.3 show less than one per cent of households in Bombay with money expenditure per capita of less than Rs 15 and 14 per cent of households spending below Rs 24, which, with any plausible cost of living adjustment must be worth more than the rural labour average of Rs 12. The figures from Bulsara on income (col. 4 of Table V. 3), show slightly more people (7 per cent) at a level of money incomes per capita in the lowest range, comparable to the rural labour households, and nearly one-quarter below Rs 25. Perhaps a maximum estimate for persons in Bombay living at similar levels to rural labourers is 20 per cent.

Another way of comparing unorganized labour incomes is by looking at wage rates rather than earnings over a period of time. Such a comparison means ignoring the possibility of differing availability of work at these wage rates, as well as all the usual difficulties of assessing the accuracy of data. The reported agricultural wage rates in Maharashtra in the second half of the sixties were mostly between Rs 2.00 and Rs 2.50 per day;[6] the daily wage on the casual labour market in Bombay was around Rs 3.00 per day. Depending on the place in question and the magnitude of the cost-of-living adjustment, real wages in the unorganized sector in Bombay seem to be somewhat above, certainly not below, most rural wage rates. It is interesting and probably significant that the highest reported wage, Rs 3.50, equalling Bombay unorganized wages even in money terms, was in Ratnagiri, the district most heavily represented as a source of migrants. Indeed, migration out of Ratnagiri towards Bombay has been so heavy that the level of population remaining in the district has almost stagnated. It is probably the shortage of local labour, caused by the migration, which has raised wage levels in this district above those generally prevailing. An alternative interpretation seems less plausible, namely that Bombay unorganized wages have been set by the earning opportunities for landless labour in a region supplying a significant (but not an overwhelming) proportion of recruits to the city's labour force. In the first place it is from places like Ratnagiri that migrants have somewhat better chances of recruitment to the Organized sector through their contacts with past migrants. Secondly, a very high proportion of Ratnagiri's inhabitants are cultivators with their own plots of land and the rural wage-labour sector is relatively small. Many of the migrants to Bombay from the district are likely to have had some rights over land too. For them the small size of holdings may have been a factor encouraging migration but for many the wage rate for agricultural labour may not have seemed relevant.

Another complication in assessing the relative economic advantages of Bombay over its hinterland is the treatment to be given to the dependency burden. On the one hand, there are fewer opportunities for women and juveniles to earn in the city than outside it; on the other hand, there are fewer of them there. Some migrants are able to avoid or reduce dependency commitments by coming to the city alone. Those who have families may be able to minimize the cost of keeping them by leaving them in the villages where they may be able to support themselves or be supported by kinsmen. In any case, money remitted to dependants in the countryside goes further than money spent on dependants in the city.

The upshot of our discussion is that, in the lower ranges, earnings in Bombay's unorganized sector are only slightly above rural earnings when we correct for differences in the cost of living. When we consider that a potential migrant to the city must take costs of moving into account and that he probably needs some compensation for risk, the real value of the differential is even further reduced. This would suggest that there is a rough equilibrating process at work bringing earnings at the bottom of the scale in Bombay into line with those of the impoverished majority outside, extending rural poverty right into the heart of this prosperous and modern city. Organized sector earnings are of course well above rural earnings and must constitute a powerful incentive to migrate for those who have the qualifications, skills or contacts to gain entry.

C. PROCESSES OF LABOUR MIGRATION

The extent of responsiveness of migration to economic conditions in the city will depend upon other features of the migration process apart from its basic economic motivation and the existence of income differentials to keep it in motion. These concern the actual processes whereby migrants come to the city and find jobs as well as the factors which determine decisions to leave. There are many different possible mechanisms of recruitment and many different versions of an individual migrant's history. We outline two stylized accounts below.

(i) Migrants may come to the city with jobs already arranged for them. This obviously applies to those who come to the city as a result of transfer by their employers. It also applies to those with relatives and friends in the city who can arrange jobs for migrants before they leave home. This advance 'fixing' of jobs will bring some people straight into the organized sector and for this type of migration, the comparison of rural with unorganized sector wages would not be relevant. Such 'job-fixing' could of course also apply to finding people places in small family firms in the unorganized sector.

(ii) Many migrants come to the city 'on spec'. Some of those who have the possibility of financial support from relatives may be prepared to be unemployed for some length of time and search for organized sector jobs. Their migration decisions would be guided not only by the differential between earnings in the organized sector and rural incomes but by the prospects of getting an organized job. Others who have no possibility of financial support or whose chances of securing organized jobs are very small would go straight into the unorganized sector from which they may 'graduate' into better-paying organized jobs after spending some time gaining experience, capital and contacts. If the unorganized sector is the point of reception, a migrant's evaluation of the advantage of coming to Bombay would take into account the remuneration in the unorganized sector together with an assessment of the probability of advancing up the ladder.[7] Out-migration is an important possibility for migrants who arrive 'on spec', if they fail to find work or to make progress out of low-paying unorganized sector jobs.

The 'contacts' hypothesis: Gore's survey provides evidence for the contention that some arrivals in the city have jobs arranged in advance. Table V. 1 quoted 74 per cent of the Marathi speaking and 82 per cent of the Hindi and Tamil speaking samples as having come to Bombay for employment reasons other than routine transfer. A breakdown of these moves is as follows:

Coming to Bombay for work	Percentage of Total Sample		
	Marathi	Hindi	Tamil
On appointment	28	4	9
With promise of a job	5	21	9
In response to an advertisement	3	3	3
With nothing definite in view	38	55	61
All non-transferees	74	82	82

Those whose jobs had been 'fixed' or promised were in a minority but a fairly sizeable one for both the Marathi and Hindi speakers. Gore attributes the high proportion of Hindi speakers informally promised jobs to the tighter-knit network of family contacts among this group, linking family members in the city with their villages in Uttar Pradesh. A majority of his sample (53 per cent of the Marathi speakers, 71 per cent of the Hindi speakers and 71 per cent of the Tamil speakers) mentioned the presence of relatives or friends as their reason for choosing Bombay rather than other possible destinations and many of these contacts had provided accommodation and help looking for work just after the migrants' arrival. In a slightly differently phrased question the Lakdawala survey had found a rather smaller proportion of the sampled migrants mentioning the presence of friends or relatives as their reasons for coming to Bombay—29 per cent 'migrants' and 27 per cent of 'displaced persons'.

Gore also found that informal contacts were not only more marked among Hindi speakers but among that part of his sample which was drawn from the employees of an old-established private sector factory. This factory did a lot of its recruiting through existing employees—a situation indicating a certain degree of paternalism in personnel policy. As the personnel officer in this factory said, 'many of the workers in unskilled jobs feel that they can bring "cousins" and friends as substitutes and go on home leave whenever it is necessary for them to do so. They seem to regard their contract with the company as transferable from them to other persons in their group.'[8] The other parts of Gore's sample were a public sector factory where more formal channels of recruitment tended to be used, and a general sample which included some unorganized workers, more of whom had come to the city 'with nothing definite in view'. Incidentally, those coming with no prior arrangement included more migrants who had left home under pressure of adverse economic conditions.

Formal channels of recruitment to organized sector jobs through the Employment Exchanges are not very well utilized. According to a survey of 67 large private sector firms employing more than 500 workers, carried out by the Directorate of Employment in 1964-5,[9] only 7 per cent of recruits were provided by the Employment Exchanges, 60 per cent by direct recruitment, 20 per cent through present employees and 13 per cent through other sources. In four surveyed public sector factories, the average picture was little different; again only 7 per cent of new recruits having been provided by the Exchange, the other sources mentioned being 65,

23 and 5 per cent respectively, although all of the recruits through existing employees were accounted for by one firm. There was also considerable variation in the proportion of recruits from this source in the private firms.

The effect of these informal networks in placing people in the city's labour market is seen in the creation of differential corridors of migration, with much heavier representation in Bombay of people from a relatively few places of origin in which migration has become a habit. Such migration corridors also give rise to specialization of migrants from different origins in different industries and occupations. This effect is shown very clearly in Visaria's survey of Ratnagiri's villages[10] which not only showed great variation in rates of out-migration between villages but a high degree of specialization in the occupations of those who had left. One village traditionally provided recruits to the armed forces, another to the police and several to the cotton mills. Such patterns are also shown, though rather less dramatically, in the more aggregated analysis of industrial affiliation by origin of worker which is carried out in Appendix V.1.

The Graduation Hypothesis : Evidence for the prevalence of this kind of migration history is rather more scanty and less conclusive. Over 80 per cent of the migrants in the Lakdawala survey remained in the same industry and occupation as they had been in when they first came to the city. Those who had changed industry were more likely to have moved out of the primary sector, construction and petty services, than out of industries. These are admittedly predominantly unorganized sectors but they only accounted for slightly more than 10 per cent of jobs on arrival. There is no way of telling whether or not there was graduation within the other industrial divisions from their unorganized to their organized sectors, since such a distinction was not made in the survey. Among occupational categories, a greater proportion of migrants had moved out of original occupations as unskilled labourers, shop assistants and small-scale retailers than those starting off in other occupations. But again those identifiably 'graduating' are relatively small in numbers. There is some further evidence from the 1961 Census compatible with the graduation hypothesis set out in Appendix V.1, but it is not very strong and other patterns also emerge.

There are some 'mixed cases' where both town-to-village information networks and graduation up the labour market occur. For instance, younger members of 'mill-hands' families on arrival in the city often first work as tiffin carriers, bringing meals to the factory; they then become 'helpers', then substitute workers (*badlis*) which finally puts them on a springboard for mill jobs. However, as recruitment to the cotton mills is slowing down, it is doubtful whether this can continue to be an important avenue of recruitment. Even in such cases, it is the influence of contacts as much as experience of work in the unorganized labour market which is in evidence.

Increasingly, recruitment to organized sector jobs requires educational qualifications. The performance of these jobs does not necessarily require formal training. Quite often, the latter simply functions as an arbitrary screening device which produces an 'over-qualified' workforce. Under these circumstances, contacts may continue to be important for securing organized sector jobs, but more experience of working in smaller enterprises in the city becomes less likely to get people places in the organized sector. It appears that the prospect of 'graduating' into organized employment applies more to people who come to the city initially for education than to those who go into work in the unorganized sector. For the latter, the relevant income comparison could well be the unorganized/rural differential discussed earlier in the chapter. The levels of remuneration in the organized sector then retain their relevance only for those with paper qualifications.

Out-migration as an element of labour market adjustment

Movement out of the city may be determined by economic conditions; people may leave when they are out of work or because their small enterprises fail. It may also be guided by the rhythms of rural life; people may return to their villages to help in sowing or harvesting. Continued contact of workers with villages is sometimes held to increase absenteeism and other difficulties for the management of industrial work but, as M.D. Morris has shown, the existence of problems of this kind was an overplayed myth even in much earlier times.[11] There could also be a problem of poor adaptation to urban work patterns if migrants only come to town for relatively short periods on the pattern of circulating migratory labour common (at least until recently) in Africa. But this practice is not very prevalent in Bombay except among the migratory construction workers.

Evidence on out-migration from the city is naturally extremely scanty because those who leave are no longer there to survey. Zachariah infers from the fact that migrants with a short duration of residence showed relatively low worker-population ratios and relatively high out-migration rates that there was some return-migration by those who failed to find jobs on coming to the city.[12] Other explanations could also fit this evidence. Those who left after a short period in the city could have been temporary migrants who had been working and the worker-population ratios could have risen with duration of residence because those who initially failed to find jobs found them later or because some of the short duration 'migrants' included visitors who were not in any case searching for work. In Gore's survey of people who were still in the city—clearly a special case in this context—11 out of 120 Hindi speaking workers and 6 out of 120 Marathi speaking workers had at some stage gone back home because they failed to find a job.[13] There is a marked contrast between the Tamil speakers from the South and the Hindi speaking migrants. Ninety-nine per cent of the Hindi speakers retained some sort of property rights in their places of birth, as against only a little over half the Tamil speakers. The Hindi speakers had a more closely knit family network stretching between city and village; most of them had left their wives and families in the village and most of them intended eventually to return there. In contrast, more of the Tamil sample had left home under adverse economic circumstances, more were working in low paying casual jobs in the unorganized sector; the majority of those who were married had their families in Bombay and a larger proportion intended to stay in Bombay after retirement.

The picture from the literature is that most migrants to Bombay spend their entire working career in the city and that out-migration takes place at retirement age. Only if migrants leave the city before they leave the labour force can one treat out-migration as a regulator of the labour supply. The likelihood of out-migration at any stage is higher for those who retain economic and social links with their places of birth. Landless labourers who migrate with their families may have nowhere to which they can return. As the proportion of women in the migration stream rises, so one might expect a fall in the eventual return migration. Indeed, in Chapter II we saw that there appears to have been a substantial drop in out-migration during the sixties. As a further conjecture, one could attribute the changing pattern of migration to increasing pressure on the land driving people towards the city. In this case the long run responsiveness of migration flows to economic conditions in urban destinations, at least taken as a whole, might be expected to diminish.

D. SOME CONCLUDING REMARKS

In this chapter we have examined the available evidence on the motivations and mechanisms of migration. Perhaps the most striking feature of migration into Bombay (and of rural-urban migration in India generally), compared to many African and Latin American cities, is that it has not reached unmanageable proportions, at any rate during the sixties. Even during the 1972 drought, most of the scarcity-affected workers were successfully diverted from the city by the rural public works programme. One pertinent contrast with African cities is that real earnings in the organized sector are stagnant. There undoubtedly exist organized/unorganized and organized/rural earnings differentials but mechanisms of recruitment are such that people are deterred from arriving simply on the off-chance of getting organized sector jobs. For most migrants, the relevant comparison is with unorganized earnings which, at the margin, are close to those outside the city. We shall return to some of these points in the next chapter but here we must emphasize another check to in-migration which is becoming increasingly important, viz. competition for scarce jobs, especially organized sector jobs, from the city-born. Already it is a live political issue manifested in the activities of the Shiv Sena and its campaign of hostility against outsiders, particularly those from the South. Extrapolation of demographic trends suggests that it might become an even more important issue in the future.

Pattern of Migrants in the Workforce: a Census Analysis

Further light is thrown on the characteristics of urban migration by some of our calculations using distributions of the economically active by migration status from the 1961 Census.[14] Tables V.4, V.5 and V.6 show concentration indices which isolate the extent to which workers with a particular migration history are over-represented among various categories of workers.[15] The analysis is confined to male migrant workers since the population of female migrants consists largely of individuals whose migration was induced by the migration of husband or father. In view of this, any economic activity on the part of female migrants is likely to be incidental to the fact that they are in the city whereas for male migrants there is more likely to be a connection between their economic activity and the reason which brought them to the city.

Table V.4 is derived from the industrial distribution of the male working population, distinguishing its place of origin. The overall distribution of workers among industries is shown at the bottom of the table and reflects the functions of the city outlined in Ch. III. Nearly half the workers are in manufacturing and most of the rest in various tertiary activities. The concentration indices show that within the overall industrial structure there is a significant degree of specialization by workers from different places of origin although the level at which categories are aggregated may disguise much detail. The breakdown of Maharashtra-born migrants by selected districts shows considerable variations in the specialization of people from different parts of the state. Over-representation of U.P. and Bihar in the primary sector probably reflects the fact that many of the city's milkmen come from U.P. This state also supplies *dhobis*, labour in the spinning departments of cotton mills and for certain tasks in the docks. Migrants from Maharashtra as well as U.P. are concentrated in division 2 which is largely the manufacture of cotton textiles. In the more sophisticated and newer manufacturing industries of division 3, largely chemicals and engineering, natives of Bombay, Kerala and Eastern India are over-represented. The highest degree of over-representation is of workers from Andhra Pradesh in Construction, where Rajasthani workers are also over-represented. The reputation of the Gujaratis in the city as a trading people is confirmed by the concentration of Gujaratis in trade and commerce. The over-representation of workers from Rajasthan, Punjab and Pakistan in trade and commerce is probably evidence of two other trading communities—Marwaris and Sindhis. Madrasis are concentrated in the transport division—probably as railway workers. The high concentrations of migrants from Kerala and Mysore in service industries is a little hard to interpret since this division covers a wide range of activities from domestic to Government service. This may reflect the concentration of the Kerala-born in clerical occupations and the Kannadigas in catering. The industrial affiliation of natives of the city is quite different from that of migrants. The most marked over-representation is in agriculture and fisheries which is not surprising since most cultivators are likely to have inherited their land and the fishermen are an indigenous community. Other industries with disproportionate numbers of the Bombay-born are Utilities (for which there is no obvious explanation) and heavy manufacturing—engineering and chemicals. The latter might be explained by natives' higher educational attainment. Zachariah has argued that some of this differential concentration in the industrial distribution of workers from different origins (and also in the similar non-uniform pattern of their occupations) can be explained by variations in the level of education of workers from different places.[16] But there remains much of the variation to be explained by place of birth, a reflection of the long-established division of labour between migrants from different places.

Tables V.5 and V.6 show the concentration of male workers with differing migration histories in various industries and categories of work status. This information can tell us something about the possible processes of graduation. There are of course limits to the extent to which this cross-sectional data could reveal migration histories. The current positions at a given moment of time of people who have been in the city for varying durations would only reveal the previous histories of those who have now completed, say, their tenth year if ten years ago this group of people had the same characteristics as those who have now freshly arrived. There are two reasons why this may not be so: (a) the opportunities which were open to the newly arrived cohort ten years ago may not be identical to those which face the new arrivals of today. This would result, among other things, from changes in the overall structure of employment. (b) Migrants in different lines of employment may not all be expected to stay in the city for similar lengths of time. Not all of the newly arrived may stay on for as much as ten years. If one finds more successful people among those with long duration of residence it does not necessarily mean that they have had to wait for their success. It could mean that those who have failed to achieve success (or perhaps never intended to look for it) have left without completing ten years' residence.

Table V.5 shows the distribution of male workers of different migration statuses over different industries. If the proportion of workers of a given migration status in any one industry were similar to that of the same migration status in the workforce as a whole (i.e. if the indices in Table V.5 were all 100) then one would be unable to detect any effect of duration of residence on industrial affiliation. We do, however, find a marked concentration of the most recent migrants in Construction (and also in Mining and Quarrying though this is too small an industry to be of much significance). The over-representation of recent migrants in Construction could be interpreted in one of two ways: (a) newly arrived migrants tend first to work in Construction before moving on to other industries or (b) Construction, in particular, draws its labour supply from a population which does not settle down in the city and in which, therefore, migrants of short duration of residence are over-represented. The latter explanation is probably the more important. The slight over-representation of recently arrived migrants in services would seem to be plausible, explained by new arrivals who later progress to other jobs, starting off as domestic servants, waiters etc. The second line of the table showing the proportion in each industry of migrants with duration between one and nine years can probably give a better idea of the industries which are easier for the newly arrived long-term migrant to break into. These moderately recent migrants are over-represented among the workers in the primary sector, Construction and Services, and slightly in heavier manufacturing. If this latter observation is at all significant, it is probably to be interpreted as the result of the age of the industry rather than of ease of entry. Longer term migrants who account for the bulk of the city's workforce are, in contrast, most heavily over-represented, though not very markedly so, in the textile and food-processing sector of manufacturing and in trade and commerce.

The industrial distribution of workers with differing duration of

residence in the city begins to give a picture of the careers of immi-
grants who graduate through the city's industrial structure as time
passes. However, there are many factors other than any process
of graduation which affect these figures. One can get another pers-
pective on the possibilities of a graduation process from information in the Census on the work-status of workers with different durations of residence. This is shown in the first four columns of Table
V.6 which also contains our rough estimates of the division of migrant employees into Organized and Unorganized, inferred from
the industrial distribution of employees. Migrant workers of one
year's duration of residence are over-represented among single
workers and, on our reckoning, among employees of the Unorganized sector. Migrants of somewhat longer duration of residence are
over-represented among employees and probably more so among
Unorganized employees. Long-duration migrants are more likely to
be employers, single workers or employees of the Organized sector.
Natives of the city are very heavily over-represented among employers and also among workers in family enterprises and are
least likely to be employees of the Unorganized sector. The association of recent arrivals with likelihood of working in the Unorganized sector seems only to apply to employees. The over-representation of single workers among both the very recent migrants and
those non-natives who have been in the city for over ten years perhaps reflects the different kinds of status of own-account workers.
The recent arrivals could be the near propertyless who set up as
street hawkers and the like and who would accept wage employment if they found it. The longer-term migrants among single workers could be the relatively prosperous craftsmen and tradesmen
who set up on their own, possibly having been employees earlier.
Family and household workers who are also part of the Unorganized sector are only over-represented among natives of the city
who have the possibility of inheriting already established enterprises
in the city. The possibilities of inheriting local enterprises would
probably also account for the very heavy over-representation of
non-migrants among employers. Although natives form only 15
per cent of the working population they account for one-third of
all employers. However, unlike the workers in family enterprises,
employers are also over-represented among the longer-term migrants who, one could argue, have had a greater opportunity to
set up their own business.

Table V. 4

Concentration of Male Workers from different Places of Birth in different Industries

Industry / Place of Birth	Index of Concentration								Male workers in all Industries	
	0 & 1 Agriculture Fisheries Forestry Mining	2 Manufacturing Mainly Textiles	3 Manufacturing Chemicals Engineering etc.	4 Construction	5 Utilities	6 Trade & Commerce	7 Transport & Communications	8 Services	as % of male workers in the city	absolute numbers
Bombay	178	83	122	73	144	109	107	80	14.7	226,151
Places outside Bombay	83	103	96	104	94	98	99	103	85.3	1,314,710
Gujarat	61	54	93	96	100	219	56	78	11.8	182,925
Mysore	28	65	108	77	56	73	98	165	5.4	83,280
Kerala	11	49	140	42	100	84	90	151	2.9	43,997
Madras	67	72	107	115	113	70	146	122	2.6	39,584
Andhra Pradesh	31	144	70	631	69	32	97	87	3.1	47,046
U.P. & Bihar	200	133	81	42	50	110	84	87	15.7	242,347
W. Bengal & Eastern States	17	63	138	46	88	81	94	138	0.5	7,360
Rajasthan & Punjab	33	51	72	292	94	161	74	120	2.9	48,665
Madhya Pradesh	44	55	97	69	50	131	123	123	0.6	9,001
Goa	11	104		31	63	45	156	126	2.1	31,838
Pakistan	17	61		96	50	193	115	98	2.8	43,359

Maharashtra	67	129	101	92	119	55	115	103	34.7	535,308
within which:										
Thana	278	102		88	88	58	110	114	1.0	15,202
Kolaba	78	110		54	19	51	101	130	3.5	53,618
Ratnagiri	61	119		96	150	48	183	110	16.6	255,927
Poona	50	111		77	50	81	162	73	3.3	50,324
Satara	39	132		58	50	61	134	67	5.2	80,736
Male Workers from all places in each industry as % of all workers	1.8	22.4	19.7	2.6	1.6	18.6	11.7	21.5	100.0	
Absolute Numbers	28,416	344,744	303,715	40,223	24,432	286,669	180,315	331,051	1,540,851	

$$\text{Index of Concentration} = \frac{\text{workers from origin } i \text{ in industry}}{\text{all workers in industry } j} \div \frac{\text{all workers from origin } i}{\text{all workers}} \times 100$$

Index > 100 signifies over-representation.

SOURCE: K. C. Zachariah *Migrants in Greater Bombay*, and *Census of India 1961*, vol. X, pt. X(1-C), Table V.

NOTE: Figures for Bombay include those born outside India and Pakistan (less than 1 per cent of the male workers) for whom separate tabulation was not available.

Table V. 5

Concentration of Male Workers of different Migration Status in different Industries

| Industry / Duration of residence | Index of Concentration | | | | | | | | | Male workers of each Migration status in All Industries | |
	0 Agriculture Fishery	1 Mining Quarrying	2 Manufacturing Textiles etc.	3 Manufacturing Heavy Industry	4 Construction	5 Utilities	6 Trade & Commerce	7 Transport & Communications	8 Services	%	absolute numbers
Migrant with duration of residence 1 year or less	153	343	65	103	281	69	69	103	132	4.64	71,527
Migrants with duration of residence 1-9 years	124	143	93	105	120	98	86	93	115	28.46	438,659
Other migrants	62	77	112	91	81	91	108	102	94	52.21	804,524
Non-Migrants	168	20	82	122	72	146	109	106	80	14.67	226,151
All male workers in each industry as % of all workers	1.7	0.1	22.4	19.7	2.6	1.6	18.6	11.7	21.5	100.00	
Absolute Numbers	24,838	1,654	344,744	303,715	40,223	24,432	286,669	180,315	331,061		1,540,891

SOURCES: *Census of India 1961*, Greater Bombay Census Tables and Special Migration Tables, and K.C. Zachariah, op. cit. for breakdown of manufacturing sector.

Table V. 6

Concentration of Male Workers of Different Migration Status by Work Status

| | Index of Concentration | | | | | | Male workers of each migration status and all work status | |
	Employers	House-hold & family workers	Single workers	Emp-loyees	Estimated Unorga-nized employees	Estimated Orga-nized employees	%	absolute numbers
Migrants with duration of residence of 1 year or less	28	85	123	101	126	87	4.64	71,527
Migrants with duration of residence of 1-9 years	31	78	93	108	124	99	28.46	438,659
Other migrants	108	96	103	99	93	102	52.21	804,524
Non-migrants	227	161	95	88	70	97	14.67	226,151
All male workers % in each work status	6.02	3.42	14.13	76.44	27.16	49.28	100.00	1,540,861
Absolute Numbers	92,746	52,653	217,648	1,177,814	418,404	759,350		

SOURCES: As for Table V.5. The estimated distribution of employees between Organized and Unorganized sectors is at best a rough approximation, which may well understate different patterns of concentration between the two sectors. For want of full information, it is based upon the industrial distribution of employees of each migration status and the proportion of the employees of each industry who appear, from Directorate of Employment figures, to be in the Organized sector. This estimate assumes that within any one industry employees of all migration statuses are equally likely to be in the Organized sector, and shows how differences in industrial affiliation alone would lead one to expect differential degrees of organized employment among workers of different migration status. The differences in membership of the Organized sector which are likely to exist within any industry—more recent migrants in the Unorganized sector—would strengthen the effect shown in columns 5 and 6.

The effects of changes in the underlying structure of the work-force and of varying lengths of completed residence should not be ignored but are less obviously disturbing to inferences about careers from Table V.6 than from the previous one. Despite these complications, the hypothesis that some migrants graduate from the low income sector to the higher income sector remains plausible. There is additional evidence to suggest that migrants improve their positions after some time in the city from the fact that their wives have generally been in the city for a shorter period and that women have low labour force participation rates once they have arrived in the city.[17] Thus the newly arrived in-migrant tends on average to be less well off than others already in the city and than he himself can hope to be later. This tendency should not be exaggerated. While the figures show certain regularities they also show that by no means all migrants of a certain category are in any particular employment situation and by no means all workers in any given employment situation have the same migration characteristics.

NOTES

1   See Ch. II for elaboration of these points.
2   For example, see M.P. Todaro, 'A Model of Labour Migration and Urban Unemployment in Less Developed Countries', *American Economic Review*, March 1969.
3   Figures for regional income per head in 1961 (from the Draft Regional Plan of Bombay Metropolitan Region 1970-71) were Rs 1,020 p.a. for Greater Bombay and Rs 313 for the rest of the state. All-India national income per head was Rs 307 at this time.
4   It is necessary to assume a spatial cost-of-living difference of this order of magnitude to reconcile the 'poverty lines' for Bombay quoted in the previous chapter with those used by other authors for India as a whole. Fonseca's 'needs-based minimum' for Bombay amounts to Rs 36 p.m. at 1961-2 prices. Dandekar and Rath calculated 'subsistence lines' (on the somewhat controversial criterion of the level of expenditure corresponding to a consumption of 2,250 calories per head per day) of Rs 14 p.m. for all rural areas, Rs 20 p.m. for rural Maharashtra and Rs 23 p.m. for all urban areas in 1961-2. See V. M. Dandekar and N. Rath, *Poverty in India* (Indian School of Political Economy, Bombay, 1971).
5   See Dandekar and Rath, op. cit.
6   See *Agricultural Wages in India* 1965-6 (Directorate of Economics and Statistics, Ministry of Food, Agriculture, Community Development and

Co-operation, Government of India, Delhi, 1968). Officially reported daily
wage rates for male field labour in various parts of Maharashtra averaged
over 12 months, ranged from Rs 1.50 to 3.50. In a few places and in a few
months rates fell below Re 1. They were higher for skilled labour (such
as carpenters) and lower for women and even lower for children. A broadly
similar if slightly higher set of figures for rural wages in the State in 1970
appears in: *Report of the Study Committee on Employment Conditions of
Agricultural Labour in Maharashtra State* (Government of Maharashtra,
July 1973).

7   This is only one possible route to 'graduation' after a time in town. Promotion occurs within the organized sector and can also occur outside it; for
example, a migrant who sets up as a shoeshiner on arrival might eventually become a shopkeeper or taxi-driver.

8   See M.S. Gore, op. cit, p. 39.

9   See the *Bombay Labour Market*, p. 84. This also shows that less than half
of all notified vacancies are actually filled by the Exchange and that many
recruits find themselves jobs through channels other than the Exchange.
The Directorate's *Monthly Progress Report*, December 1970, suggests
that, in general, public sector employers are much more likely to use
the Exchanges. At a time when there were 752 Public Sector establishments
(not necessarily identical with employers) the Directorate recorded 322
Public Sector employers using the Exchanges as against 358 private
employers and 2,546 private establishments.

10 P.M. Visaria, 'The Pattern of Out-migration from Coastal Maharashtra
in India' (mimeo., Bombay and Princeton Universities, 1969).

11 See Morris D. Morris, *The Emergence of an Industrial Labour Force in
India* (University of California Press, 1965).

12 Zachariah, op. cit., p. 100 and p. 217.

13 Gore, op. cit., p. 68.

14 The use of concentration analysis enables us to talk about the characteristics
of those members of a given group of workers who make the total group
distinct from other groups. Those who differentiate the group from others
are treated as characteristic of the group though they may not necessarily
be in the majority.

15 The proportion of particular origin of all workers in a particular industry
can easily be calculated by multiplying the concentration index by the
corresponding percentage figures in the penultimate column. The proportion
in a particular industry of all workers of one particular origin is the product
of the concentration index and the percentage figure in the penultimate
row. Similar considerations apply in the other two tables where the migration category changes to duration of residence and the economic classification to work-status.

16 Zachariah, op. cit., p. 251 and p.317.

17 P.M. Visaria, 'The Working Force in Maharashtra State' (mimeo., Bombay
University, 1969).

CHAPTER SIX

ECONOMIC POLICY AND THE EMPLOYMENT PROBLEM

This book is inspired by the belief that economic policy in India has given insufficient attention to the absorption and productive utilization of the very abundant supplies of labour in the country. As a result, production has suffered and the incomes of a large section of the population have stagnated at a miserable level. We have concentrated on the urban dimension of this problem, using Bombay as a case-study. Earlier chapters have analysed demographic trends in the city; the size, composition and growth of the organized and unorganized sectors; relative incomes in the two sectors; and the role of migration as a link between the city and the rest of the country. The available evidence makes it plain that at least half the workforce in this leading Indian city is to be found in unorganized activities and that the expansion of the organized sector has been too slow to reduce their numbers absolutely or proportionately. The disparity in standards of living between the two sectors highlights the disturbing nature of these trends. It points to the conclusion that the number of people excluded from the relatively privileged part of the economy is rapidly increasing.[1] It is clear that these developments are not unique to Bombay but parallel those in the rest of the country. This chapter examines the policy issues raised by these developments in greater detail. We begin with policy issues at the national level and then proceed to consider certain specifically urban problems. Inevitably, the terrain is controversial. The range of our empirical work is too narrow to permit any easy conclusions to be drawn even for Bombay, let alone for the country as a whole. The available evidence is, however, sufficient to indicate that a profound re-thinking of economic policy is required.

A. THE CHARACTER OF ECONOMIC DEVELOPMENT IN INDIA

It is clear, taking a retrospective view, that the philosophy and conduct of Indian economic policy aggravated the employment problem. This was not the unavoidable consequence of a fast-growth strategy. There are examples of both capitalist and socialist developing countries which have managed to combine rapid growth with fuller mobilization of labour. Why then did India fail in this respect?

To some extent, this failure followed from the undue emphasis on capital-intensive techniques of production and on heavy industry, both of which were believed to be essential for rapid economic growth. The presumed superiority of capital-intensive methods was based on the idea that they would generate bigger investible surpluses than labour-intensive methods. In fact, this outcome depends on certain assumptions, not always fulfilled in practice. The belief in capital-intensive techniques was carried further to the conclusion that India should set up first, second and third generation capital-goods industries. This strategy largely ignored the possibilities of foreign trade. Even if it is accepted that capital-intensity is desirable, it does not logically follow that the capital goods and machine tools required have to be *domestically* manufactured. It might have been more economical in terms of the nation's resources to concentrate more on export markets and to import some of the capital goods. Given relative factor proportions and cost conditions as between India and the developed countries, greater export orientation could have achieved higher output and employment without sacrificing growth.

In practice, the insulation from foreign trade was carried much further than the setting up of capital goods industries. Import-substitution in a wide range of consumer goods was permitted or encouraged, many of them heavily capital-using. Thus, the organized industrial sector came to acquire the characteristics of an enclave using 'modern' techniques to produce 'modern' products catering to middle and upper income groups, but with relatively low employment potential. The elaborate structure of licencing and controls which evolved with the stated purpose of pre-empting scarce resources for 'essential' purposes ended up by subsidizing this privileged modern sector. The harshness of this regime for those who did not participate in it was not tempered to any significant degree by measures to redistribute incomes or assets. The rhetoric of the Plans included references to the need for land reform, community development and rural public works. In fact, efforts in this direction were thoroughly half-hearted. The distribution of resources in agriculture remained highly skewed, the taxation of the rural rich remained negligible and there were signs that the potential benefits from the major technological breakthroughs in agriculture would be usurped by the larger farmers to the detriment of the vast majority of smallholders and landless labourers. It is not surprising then to find that in the last two decades the number of people below the 'poverty line' did not fall, and in the opinion of some scholars, increased substantially.

Rapid growth calls for high rates of saving and investment. This truth was not given sufficient emphasis in our policy-making. On the other hand, the half-truth that rapid growth requires concentration on capital-intensive methods and products was over-emphasized. We do not wish to imply that India should not have a capital goods industry or that there should be a wholesale move towards labour-using techniques. We do not wish to assert that there has been no economic progress in India or that there have been no external constraints on our Planners in the form of wars, droughts and the capriciousness of aid donors. We are arguing, however, that a change of emphasis in the direction of fuller and more productive utilization of labour is now badly needed together with efforts to increase savings. Such a change would contribute to improving the *use* of savings and the *distribution* of consumption; matters in which our performance so far has been sadly out of tune with our objectives.[2]

B. POLICIES TOWARDS THE EMPLOYMENT PROBLEM

The employment problem, in the broad sense in which we are using the term, arises from the pressure of numbers on a dual economy. Labour productivity is high within the enclave-like organized sector and those lucky to participate in its benefits enjoy a relatively high standard of living. From the national point of view, however, it contributes on the one hand to a waste of production potential owing to misallocation of human and non-human resources and on the other hand to a worsening of the distribution of income by the exclusion of those outside it from its benefits. Policies to arrest these trends may conveniently, if rather artificially, be divided into two groups: a) Employment Creation Policies which shift low productivity labour to jobs with higher productivity and b) Resource Distribution Policies which shift resources towards workers in existing low productivity jobs.

(a) *Employment Creation Policies*

The motivation of these policies is to employ labour which has low opportunity cost in more productive occupations. Such labour includes the un-and under-employed and also 'the working poor'. If successful, these policies would increase aggregate output and at the same time make possible an increase in the incomes of those newly employed. The possibilities for such productive increases in employment exist both within the organized sector and outside it and involve changes in techniques of production and the pattern of output.

The Organized Sector: Techniques and Products

The employment potential of organized industry with *existing* techniques is extremely limited. It is often asserted that the scope for *changing* techniques is also non-existent but this is much too pessimistic. Even the 'core' of a process exhibits totally fixed coefficients only in some 'flow' industries like petrochemicals. In many engineering industries, whether to have assembly lines, automatic machinery and so on is a matter of choice. Construction is characterized by a good deal of technical flexibility; so are many ancilliary activities in any industry. In addition, there are possibilities of inventing new and more appropriate techniques by suitably directed research and of using techniques which, though not 'modern' by developed countries' standards, are better suited to factor availabilities in the country. Another widely prevalent aspect of excessive capital-intensity in India is the under-utilization of installed capacity.[3] Multi-shift work would seem to be an obvious need in industry to increase employment and output, and to economize on capital. The demand for labour also depends on the composition of output. This could be changed over time in a labour-using direction and there are good arguments for doing so in the Indian situation

Encouraging extra employment in the organized sector requires appropriate incentives. For several years organized industry has enjoyed heavy protection from foreign competition, subsidized capital and sellers' markets. These policies cannot indefinitely be justified on 'infant industry' grounds. It is not sufficiently realized that the ultra-high protection of organized industry exacerbates the employment problem. Greater exposure to international markets would, on balance, increase the demand for labour by increasing the profitability of labour-intensive techniques and products. We are not arguing for an immediate move to untrammelled free trade. Departures from free trade are justified because of India's large weight in certain primary product markets and also because protection is the only feasible means of correcting the bias against industry created by various market imperfections. However, these reasons cannot possibly justify the existing policy of indiscriminate protection through import controls. The other side of the coin of heavy import-substitution is the continuing discrimination against exports (in spite of the haphazard subsidy schemes which are in force). Even organized industrial wage rates in India are fully competitive with those abroad and it is indeed incredible that we should not be able to have the rapid growth rates in exports of labour-intensive manufactured products that some other developing countries seem to have managed with ease. The incentive is lacking: it is very much more comfortable and profitable to sell in home markets.[4] A vigorous programme of export promotion could contribute significantly to productive employment creation.

An argument is sometimes advanced against even the gradual and moderate trade liberalization that is suggested here to the effect that international trade is bad because it has strong 'demonstration effects' encouraging the consumption of Western-style luxury goods. We would agree entirely that such consumption should be prevented but that is surely to be managed by prohibiting domestic production *and* imports rather than by prohibiting imports alone. A good deal of industrial output in India caters to the luxury consumption of the upper income groups and is both import-intensive and capital intensive. Many of these goods have 'excessive' standards in the sense that they over-fulfil the needs that they are intended to satisfy. From the viewpoint of social welfare, it may be better to have the same needs fulfilled by different goods. The point applies to both traded and non-traded goods. Cotton shirts may be preferable to drip-dry shirts and soap to detergents. Excessive standards could be reduced in residential construction and medicine. We would certainly favour changing the pattern of consumption in the Indian economy in a more 'appropriate' labour-using direction through suitable taxes.[5] (This, however, is not as easy to do as might appear at first sight. Every shift away from luxury consumption would not necessarily increase the demand for labour. For example, domestic service is an important item in the spending of the rich. The whole matter requires careful investigation.) The measures advocated above would also encourage some unorganized industries. Export-oriented policies would promote handicrafts which already employ substantial numbers. The reduction of excessive standards of 'quality' in consumption would make it easier for many unorganized producers to compete.[6] This process would be further helped if the government encouraged sub-contracting of actually or potentially labour-intensive operations by the organized sector to unorganized producers and if it could itself set an example in this respect. However, these measures would not, in general, suffice without resource distribution policies which we discuss later.

The under-utilization of capacity in organized industry is a complex phenomenon. To some extent, it is related to the existence of sellers' markets and the distorted system of rationing foreign exchange. The curious policy of making foreign exchange allocations in proportion to capacity naturally encourages those who can manipulate the system to over-capitalize. In some industries, there are far too many plants in relation to demand. ('Regional balance' is one reason for this but it can obviously be carried too far.) What this means is that fewer larger-scale plants would save capital and thus make it possible to increase employment elsewhere. In other industries, multi-shift working would be profitable if there were more competition; given the existing sellers' markets, the inconvenience of supervising and organizing it outweighs the gains from doing so as far as managers are concerned. Trade union rules too do not favour multi-shift work. Another employment-increasing change would be to reduce the length of shifts. This would make it possible to spread the benefits of employment wider. Changes such as these are not easy and would require active government intervention to force both management and trade unions to look beyond the interests of those already employed.[7]

Agriculture

We now turn to agriculture which is where any programme of

increased labour absorption must concentrate. No feasible growth of organized industry, even allowing for changes in techniques and products, could by itself make a significant dent in the employment problem. The vast majority of the Indian labour force has to survive in agriculture and so will most of the new entrants to the labour force. A crucial element in attacking the employment problem is land reform whch is more properly included in the category of resource-distribution policies. However, employment creation policies do have a very important role to play, both positive and negative. The positive role is connected with rural public works. A comprehensive rural works programme geared to building up the infrastructure—irrigation, land improvement, roads—that agriculture so desperately needs would transform the Indian countryside, especially if coordinated with land redistribution and consolidation.[8] The potential of such a programme for providing productive employment to very large numbers of people is beyond doubt. The constraints on the programme are those of resources and organization. Workers on rural public projects would have to be paid and the resulting demand for wage-goods satisfied by an expansion of supply or a reduction in demand from other sources. The expansion in supply consequent upon the projects themselves cannot be immediate. On the other hand, to the extent that the Green Revolution is already increasing marketable surpluses in some areas and crops, the problem of creating a wage fund is eased. In theory, the need for a wage fund could be avoided altogether if workers were to agree to be paid *after* the output of the projects on which they are employed actually materializes. This is the basis on which family farms often work, and in principle, there is no reason why cooperative groups larger than the family should not work on the same lines. Chinese communes and Israeli kibbutzim are possible examples and in the longer run they are options which may be seriously considered. In the immediate future, however, it would be foolhardy to expect that a major rural works programme could be put into effect without extra taxation. The potential clearly exists for extra taxation of the rural rich and of the beneficiaries of the Green Revolution generally but at the moment it is equally evident that the political will is lacking. Management and organization are also important problems. An integrated package of productive projects has to be conceived and coordinated and this cannot be done without much local knowledge. It is also a matter of some complexity to give appropriate guidelines to local project managers which would enable them to select the right projects.[9]

The negative aspect of employment-creation policies in agriculture is to prevent labour displacement, a dangerous possibility associated with recent technological breakthroughs. On balance, the availability of the new seeds should increase the demand for labour. Yields are higher, so more labour is required for harvesting and threshing; in addition, the increase in yields depends on various careful operations such as seed-bed preparation and weeding. If multiple cropping is possible, then the demand for labour increases even more. These increases in labour requirements are likely to outweigh considerably the reduction in labour requirements from the increased efficiency of complementary inputs such as water and fertilizers. However, these favourable employment effects could be partially frustrated if the larger capitalist farmers substitute labour by machinery. There are understandable reasons for the perceived private advantages of using tractors, mechanical threshers and even combine harvesters. Their nuisance value is less than that of men or animals, their prices are low or subsidized (in relation to the true cost of producing and importing them) and they are items of conspicuous consumption. From the social point of view, however, it is clear that mechanization in agriculture must be very carefully controlled. Mechanization is sometimes defended on the ground that it makes it easier to have multiple cropping which requires precise timing and quick completion of various seasonal operations. But this would seem to indicate the need for research into developing light machinery which can alleviate specific seasonal labour bottlenecks rather than for equipment which substitutes for labour over the whole year. At a more fundamental level, it could be argued that the growth of capitalist agriculture should itself be arrested. Though, in some regions, capitalist farms have been very dynamic, there are reasons to believe that their employment and output per acre are lower than those of family farms. One possible reason for this is that the supply price of labour is lower when a man is working for himself and his immediate family. If family sympathy could be preserved in larger cooperative groups, they too would show the advantages of family farms without the diseconomies of small size. In the long run, therefore, employment policies cannot be divorced from fundamental questions of social and economic organization.[10]

(b) Resource Distribution Policies

The rationale for such policies is quite straightforward. Many of the 'working poor' are to be found in low productivity occupations and many of them are self-employed. The potential for shifting them into the organized sector is limited. Techniques in the organized sector are not indefinitely flexible and the relatively high wages in this sector constrain the growth of employment. Specially devised employment programmes are possible but the number of productive projects is not unlimited and the organizational difficulties are formidable. On the other hand, there is reason to believe that the low productivity of the 'working poor' is not the result of any inherent inefficiency on their part but simply of their lack of resources and technology.

An important step forward would be quite simply to eliminate the bias in the existing system against unorganized producers. The pre-emption by the organized sector of cheap credit, foreign exchange and essential raw materials makes it more difficult and expensive for unorganized producers to obtain them.[11] If this bias were eliminated and sub-contracting encouraged, the unorganized sector could become highly competitive in both export and home markets as far as certain labour-intensive industrial operations are concerned. In agriculture too it is essential that small farmers should find it easier to secure various inputs. One of the merits of the Green Revolution is supposed to be that it is neutral with respect to scale. Good results with the new seeds require various complementary inputs such as water and fertilizers, and in principle these divisible inputs could be provided to even the smallest farms. In practice, however, farmers have unequal access to all these inputs and to credit and technical know-how as well. Ending this discrimination could raise output and incomes on many small farms. Government policies towards unorganized producers in urban areas are also unnecessarily restrictive. For example, many of them have to obtain licences to set up their business whether they are street traders, carpenters or taxi-drivers.[12] In many cases, these licences have very little to do with any objectives of public policy such as the maintenance of health standards. They simply encourage a black-market in licences and add to the existing risks of investment in unorganized activities the additional risk of being on the wrong side of the law or at the mercy of a corrupt official. Basically, the authorities have to revise their image of the unorganized sector as a motley collection of riff-raff with little productive potential.[13]

The presumed 'efficiency' of organized, modern activities compared to unorganized, traditional activities may be only an illusion based on a price structure distorted by inappropriate subsidies and controls, including those on foreign trade and the privileged access of the organized sector to political influence. The economic characteristics of the unorganized sector deserve to be carefully studied. It is probably a complex mixture of efficient and inefficient activities and a policy of selective help would therefore have to be devised.[14] Ensuring parity for unorganized producers as suggested above may not go far enough and may not be effective without active measures to channel resources in their direction and to alter the distribution of new asset creation in their favour. Public control of the banking system would have a major role to play in the formulation of suitable criteria for loans. Carefully scrutinized redirection of newly mobilized savings through the credit mechanism towards unorganized producers would be a way of building up productive assets in their hands over time. 'Productive assets' must obviously be taken to include technology and skills. The role of the government is crucial in promoting the development and dissemination of appropriate technologies and in spreading the benefits of the right kind of education. As far as the distribution of *existing* assets (as distinguished from *new* assets) is concerned, this is in some cases physically impossible and in most cases politically very sensitive. A major asset where the constraints on redistribution are principally political is land. Nonetheless land redistribution is of major significance in solving the employment problem in agriculture.[15]

C. OBJECTIVES, TRADE-OFFS AND CONSTRAINTS

The case advanced in the previous section may sound too good to be true. It might be objected that the policies of employment creation and resource distribution would, given realistic constraints, make it more difficult in comparison with present policies to increase output and to spread the benefits of development to the poor. We discuss some of the relevant issues below.[16] The reader may note that we shall use the term *employment policies* as a shorthand expression to cover both employment creation and resource distribution policies.

(a) *Employment Policies and Aggregate Output*

From the production point of view, the rationale of employment policies is that they eliminate the waste of productive potential. It may be feared, however, that they would do the opposite. For example, public works of the 'digging holes to fill them up' variety may do so. Even if we assume that the opportunity cost of labour is zero, the materials and capital equipment used on a project would have alternative uses, thus reducing total output below what it would otherwise be. Resource distribution policies may lead to similar results. It is feared, for example, that the unorganized sector uses *inferior* techniques, meaning thereby techniques which use more of all factors of production per unit of output than other known techniques. In so far as this is true, diverting resources to the unorganized sector would reduce aggregate output.

Assertions about the inferiority of techniques in the unorganized sector are not always based on hard evidence. One suspects that in many cases the 'evidence' consists of nothing more than the greater commercial profitability of 'modern' techniques. But this may be the result (a) of the existing relative prices of outputs which are a function, among other things, of the existing unequal distribution of income and (b) of the existing imperfections in factor markets which, on balance, favour the organized sector using 'modern' techniques. A proper test of 'inferiority' would require that the *physical* requirements of different techniques in producing the *same* output be compared. Very few studies of this type exist and more research on this subject is urgently required. Going further, even if certain techniques are proved to be inferior, the return to research on the invention of new labour-using but non-inferior techniques may be very high. Going still further, it may under certain extreme circumstances be desirable to divert resources to even genuinely inferior activities because that happens to be the only feasible means of redistributing incomes.

We would not, on the whole, set much store by this last point. In practice, redistribution is easier if output is growing than if it is shrinking. The danger of indiscriminate employment policies leading to adverse effects on output is a real one and must be guarded against. Hence it is important in the field of public works to take great care in the identification and selection of projects and in the choice between 'modern' and 'traditional' activities to appreciate the importance of economies of scale in modern industry.

(b) Employment Policies and Growth

A standard argument against employment policies is that even if they increase current output they would reduce the *growth* of output. Such an outcome is possible if employment policies increase current consumption more than current output and if the resulting negative effect on saving and investment cannot be counteracted by fiscal measures. Since the government is concerned about the welfare of future generations this is obviously a question of some importance.

To make the point in the most transparent manner, consider the argument for employment creation in the public sector where the real wage is set by trade unions and is inflexible downward. Assume, for simplicity, that wages are entirely consumed and that the surplus of output over wages is used for investment. Assume further that the opportunity cost of employing labour is zero in terms of output sacrificed elsewhere. Now, if the government were concerned solely about maximizing current output, any increase in employment which contributes positively to output is justified. However, if the government is also concerned about the growth of output it cannot ignore the effects of extra employment on the investible surplus. If the government is already using its taxation powers to the hilt, extra employment at fixed wages would begin to have a negative effect on the surplus well before output is maximized. The optimal amount of employment then depends on the value of investment relative to current consumption. The higher the premium on investment, the smaller is the desirable level of employment for any given real wage; for any given premium on investment, the lower the real wage, the higher is the desirable level of employment. The above argument applies equally to organized private sector enterprises if the marginal propensity to save out of profits is higher than that out of wages. In that case, increasing employment beyond the level freely chosen by entrepreneurs faced by given wage rates, through say subsidies on labour-use, would increase output and consumption of the employed but reduce profits and savings. A similar argument could also apply to resource-distribution policies if they change the distribution of income in favour of those, say unorganized producers, with lower saving propensities at the margin.[17]

The importance of this line of argument cannot be denied. There is a real danger, however, of people being over-impressed by it.

It would be useful, therefore, to examine the assumptions on which it rests in order to assess its relevance for economic policy-making in India.

(i) The argument assumes that the government is operating under a saving constraint. While no government can be expected to have total fiscal control over the economy, it is reasonable enough to doubt whether the Indian government is exploiting its taxation potential fully. To the extent that it is not, the premium on investment would be lower and the argument against employment policies that much weaker.

(ii) The premium on investment also depends on the social preference between present and future consumption.
India's performance in relieving poverty is so dismal that it could be argued that the government should worry some-what more about consumption today and somewhat less about consumption tomorrow. In other words, the implicit discount rate and premium on investment have arguably been excessively cruel towards those who have already been born.

(iii) The argument assumes that employment policies would increase output less than current consumption because they shift the distribution of income from high to low savers. It may be true that corporations save more than industrial workers. It is not clear that large landowners have higher saving propensities than small farmers. The evidence here needs careful examination.

(iv) If the economy is not operating on the 'production frontier' and if employment policies enable it to do so, output, current consumption and savings could *all* increase so that no trade-off arises. Many economists have suggested that greater exposure to international markets, for example, would have this effect.

(v) The argument appears to be against all employment creation. This needs careful interpretation. It is true that the employment of labour at any wage rate above its alternative product could have a negative impact on the investible surplus. However, as between two equally productive activities, this negative impact is lower, the lower is the wage rate. Thus, the practical thrust of the argument is not against all em-

ployment creation but against employment creation at particularly *high* wage rates.

(c) *Employment Policies and Equality*

Though the literature on this subject has not emphasized this
issue, employment policies could under certain circumstances have
adverse consequences not only for equality between generations
but also for equality among contemporaries.[28] Consider again
for simplicity the organized public sector where the real wage is
fixed and higher than the alternative product of labour. Assume
that the surplus of output over wages (which are entirely consumed)
is used by the government to subsidize the incomes of the very
poor. If employment at given wages were expanded, output would
increase and so would the incomes of those who secure employment, but the redistributable surplus would decline. Optimizing the
volume of employment then involves weighing up the positive welfare value of the increased potential incomes of those who would
be employed against the negative welfare-value of the reduction in
potential incomes of those towards whom the surplus could be
redistributed. The higher the rate at which the social marginal
utility of income declines with increasing income (i.e. the greater the
value placed on equality), the smaller the extent to which it is desirable to expand organized employment. The same argument would
apply to employment creation in the private organized sector since
profits can be taxed and used for redistribution. It would also apply
to any resource-distribution policies which reduce the government's
tax take. In fact, this line of argument is entirely symmetric with the
previous one about growth, the only difference being that it is concerned with income distribution between contemporaries rather
than between generations. Again, its practical thrust is not against
employment creation as such but against excessive employment
creation in relatively high-wage activities. Note that the many
qualifications mentioned in discussing the preceding argument
against employment creation apply *mutatis mutandis* to this argument as well.

(d) *The Social Opportunity Cost of Labour*

The various considerations which bear on the decision concerning
the desirability of extra employment can be given formal expression
in the language of economic theory through the concept of the

'social opportunity cost of labour' or the 'shadow wage'. This is the *social* cost of employing an extra man, taking account of the objectives of society and the constraints, technological and political, on the achievement of these objectives. Particular attention was focused earlier in this section on social preferences concerning redistribution between contemporaries and between generations and the political/ fiscal constraints which prevent the achievement of the 'first best solution' which would be feasible if technological constraints alone were binding.

The particular question we have concentrated on can be reformulated as follows: How should labour be priced from the social point of view (or what is the shadow wage of labour) in evaluating projects where the real wage which workers are actually paid is institutionally or politically determined and is higher than their alternative marginal product? If the government were free to vary income distribution independently of production, the shadow wage would be equal to the alternative marginal product of labour; hence, employment in the activities under consideration should be expanded till the marginal product of labour falls to the level prevailing outside. Given the political/fiscal constraints, however, the government lacks the freedom mentioned and in this situation the shadow wage is, in general, higher and optimal employment lower than in the absence of these constraints.

In principle, the shadow wage for any period, along with shadow prices for other commodities and resources, can be computed only by solving a general equilibrium inter-temporal maximization problem. But more rough-and-ready methods can also be used. In the Theoretical Appendix to this chapter we derive an expression for the shadow wage, taking account of both inter-temporal and intra-temporal considerations, under certain simplified assumptions. The analysis suggests that with the organized/unorganized earnings differentials prevailing in Bombay, the shadow wage would be about 80 per cent of organized sector earnings; in other words, that in appraising projects in the organized sector, labour should be priced at 80 per cent of its apparent cost or, equivalently, that a labour subsidy of 20 per cent would be justified *on this count*. The Appendix also provides theoretical support for the assertion earlier in this section that the argument against employment creation is weaker, the lower the wages that have to be paid to newly employed workers. This would suggest, *ceteris paribus*, that employment creation in rural public works, for example, is socially preferable to employment creation in organized industry. The Appendix also examines the sensitivity of the optimal rate of labour subsidy for organized activities to variations in the organized/unorganized earning differential. Though the relationship turns out to be non-monotonic, it can be shown that a case for paying lower rates of labour subsidy to activities which have higher differentials can be established for plausible values of relevant parameters.

The shadow wage also depends on considerations other than social preferences towards income distribution. A very important consideration in the urban context is the possibility of migration in response to job creation in urban areas. We take up this issue in the next section; it is also discussed in the Theoretical Appendix.

D.   URBAN PROBLEMS

The foregoing discussion has indicated the benefits and costs of employment policies at the national level. We now proceed to discuss certain specifically urban problems. Employment creation policies in urban areas raise special problems of their own because they can, under certain circumstances, lead to excessive rural-urban migration. Such migration, it is feared, could reduce rural output, accentuate regional imbalances, worsen the environmental problems associated with urbanization and exacerbate political unrest in urban areas.

(a) *The Migration Question*

In some quarters, it is held that rural-urban migration is a blind and inexorable flood which cannot be prevented by any feasible policy.[19] This view we take to be contrary to both common-sense and evidence. Chapter V has provided some information supporting the view that migration is principally a response to employment and income opportunities. The question which is both important and difficult to answer is *how* sensitive it is to changes in these conditions. The question is important because the answer affects the type of employment policies that should be pursued, and whether their thrust should be in urban or rural areas.

The problem with employment creation in the organized sector in urban areas can be set out most dramatically by employing a simple model. Suppose that all employment in urban areas is in the organized sector, the rest of the urban labour force being openly unemployed; and that there is full employment in rural areas in the sense that anyone who is willing to work can do so at the going wage. Assume that the urban organized sector wage (w) is inflexible downwards (say as a result of trade union pressure or wage legislation) and higher than the rural wage (m) which is approximately constant in the face of labour withdrawal because of the relative size of the rural sector. If urban wages were flexible, then migration would proceed till urban wages were brought to equality with those in the countryside. Since urban wages cannot fall, the burden of equilibration is thrown on to the rate of urban employment. A potential migrant would move to the city if his *expected* earnings there are higher than the rural income he would forego. Migration would proceed till, in equilibrium.

$$m = pw,$$

where p, the probability of getting a job, is inversely related to the extent of unemployment. If $pw > m$ migration would increase, increasing unemployment thereby reducing p and vice versa. It is clear that with m and w both fixed, the equilibrium value of p is determined. So for every extra job created, the urban labour force would increase by that quantity which would keep p constant. To get a precise answer to the migration response from the creation of an extra urban job one must postulate a definite relationship between p and the employment variables. The simplest such relationship is that p equals employment divided by the labour force. (This would be true, for example, if workers were hired on a random basis every day). Thus we can write

$$p = \frac{E}{L}$$

where E is employment and L the labour force, $(L-E)$ being the number unemployed. Now consider the effects of creating an extra job in the organized sector. Denoting the migration response by z it follows from our assumptions that

$$p = \frac{E}{L} = \frac{E+1}{L+Z}$$

Solving for z, we have $z = L/E$. Thus, for every extra job, the urban labour force would increase by L/E of which $(L/E - 1)$ would *add* to the pool of urban unemployment. There is a further serious implication of this simple model if we proceed on the assumption that rural and urban wages equal the respective marginal products of labour.

The orthodox theory of resources allocation suggests that labour should be transferred from low to high productivity occupations. However, in the above situation the creation of an extra job increases industrial product by w but reduces rural product by $m(L/E)$ which is exactly equal to w, since $m=(E/L)w$. Thus, employment creation would appear to lead to no gain at all, in marked contrast to the orthodox view. The shadow wage or social opportunity cost of employment would be w even though the rural marginal product is only m.[20]

If this model were taken to be a good approximation to reality, it would follow that increased organized employment in urban areas such as Bombay should be strongly discouraged. Before judging the relevance of the model, it is important to investigate how the unorganized sector can be incorporated into it. This question is important because in Bombay (and very probably in other Indian cities as well) the overwhelming majority of the non-organized labour force is engaged in the unorganized sector rather than being openly unemployed. To incorporate the unorganized sector into the model, imagine the potential migrant as having not only a chance, p, of entering the organized sector but also the certainty of being employed in the casual unorganized labour market in which wages denoted by n are flexible. Assume that being employed in the unorganized labour market does not impede searching for organized sector jobs so that there is no point in being openly unemployed. In equilibrium then, $m=pw+(1-p)n$. Since, by assumption, $w>m$ and $0<p<1$, it follows that $n<m$. In other words, the urban unorganized wage would be *lower* than the rural wage. The commonsense of this result is that a potential migrant, at the margin, is willing to accept the certainty of a lower wage in the unorganized sector for some chance of a higher wage in the organized sector. In this case, again, if factor payments are equal to marginal products, the shadow wage is equal to w.[21]

Though this model is a theoretical possibility, it does not seem to be particularly realistic in the case of Bombay. Evidently, rigorous testing of the model is impossible with the data at hand. However, the implication of the model that $n<m$ can be tested against the available evidence. The data we have presented in Chapter V do not suggest that unorganized urban earnings are lower than rural earnings, even after adjusting for the higher cost of living in the city. On the contrary, they definitely indicate that unorganized

earnings are roughly equal if not higher than rural earnings.[22] This finding suggests the hypothesis that migration brings n and m into equality and that w does not enter into the calculations of potential migrants. This could be justified on one or two grounds; in fact, both probably have some relevance. The first ground is that migration does not improve a man's chance of getting an organized sector job. If recruitment takes place purely through contacts and if contacts are not improved by coming to the city, then the probability of a man's getting an organized sector job is either one or zero depending upon whether he has someone who can effectively 'speak for him' or not. The second ground is that the stream of migrants consists of two non-competing groups: the educated and the uneducated. The latter have a negligible chance of getting an organized sector job in the absence of contacts because in the presence of an excess supply of applicants, organized sector employers use education as a screening device in selecting people. So the calculations of the uneducated consist entirely of comparing urban unorganized and rural opportunities. The educated migrants compete for jobs in the organized sector along with educated natives and it is among them that open unemployment would be concentrated. Further, since migrants are, on the whole, less educated than the city-born, it would follow that open unemployment would be largely an intra-urban phenomenon.

It is possible to set up different models based on varying assumptions; interpreting the situation in Bombay is more difficult. A good deal of information in Chapter V suggests that migrants obtain jobs through contacts. For example, there is a significant degree of specialization within the overall industrial structure of workers from different states of origin. More impressionistic evidence confirms that workers in particular organized sector occupations are drawn from particular districts, even from particular villages. The existence of such migration 'corridors' and the importance of 'clan contacts' has also been confirmed by cross-section econometric studies of migration relationships.[23] This evidence does not by itself refute the hypothesis that people migrate in response to *expected* income differences with the corollary that the migration response to the creation of organized jobs may be much larger than the number of extra jobs created. It could be that each occupation has its own pool of 'applicants' to draw upon from among whom a random choice is made and that the 'expected income' mechanism works within each 'pool' or 'corridor'. However, some information (discussed in Chapter V) suggests, in addition, that many workers have jobs 'fixed up' for them *before* they migrate. If this were a widely prevalent case it would be incompatible with the corollary of the 'expected income' explanation of migration mentioned above. There is also some evidence (admittedly rather weak) to suggest that migrants are less well-educated than the city-born and that open unemployment rates are lowest among illiterates, indicating that open unemployment could be mainly an intra-urban phenomenon.[24] On the other hand, some evidence is also present to indicate that some migrants 'graduate' from the unorganized to the organized sector.

All this points to the conclusion that migration patterns in Bombay are complex, not to be summarized neatly by any simple model. But the extreme hypothesis that job creation in the organized sector is self-defeating because of the severity of the migration response must surely be viewed with suspicion. This extreme hypothesis does not really accord with common-sense, in any case. The simple migration models discussed above ignore *differences* between migrants. Migrants would differ in the incomes they would forego, their prospects of finding jobs at urban destinations, the value they put on the monetary gain from organized sector employment and in their willingness to take risks. What this amounts to is that the marginal cost of being an 'applicant' for an organized sector job rises as the number of applicants increases. The migration response would therefore depend on the elasticity of this cost curve and there is no *a priori* reason to expect it to be quantitatively very high.[25] Research into measuring the elasticity of this cost curve in Bombay would be very valuable. We have argued in this book that the elasticity is low but largely on the basis of 'casual empiricism'.

It would be wrong to conclude from all this that India's 'employment problem' can be solved in urban areas. The main thrust of employment policies would have to be in rural areas. But employment creation in the urban organized sector *can* play a part, though a minor one and extreme pessimism about the influx of migrants that would be prompted by increased organized sector employment is unjustified. What about resource distribution policies to encourage the unorganized sector? Again, if these measures were undertaken only in the cities and opened up a significant gap between urban and rural incomes there would be an income-equalizing migration response. However, as will be indicated further below, the magnitude of this response will depend upon the *type* of unorganized activities which are encouraged.

(b) *Costs and Benefits of Urbanization*

Whether employment policies should be pursued in a particular urban area is a complex question depending on many different considerations. In formulating a national employment policy, alternatives must be carefully considered so that the best *distribution* of employment opportunities is achieved.

An important underlying issue is the optimal location of economic activity. This depends on the spatial distribution of natural resources, unit costs of production at different centres (inclusive of the cost of providing the relevant infra-structure), relative costs of transporting raw materials and finished goods to and from various centres, the spatial pattern of demand and the objectives of society. In calculating costs of production, due attention must be given to the possibilities of achieving 'economies of agglomeration' which arise from having concentrations of economic activity. For example, concentrations of industry may make labour training facilities cheaper. The presence of a large trading network may reduce the need to carry large inventories. There are economies in providing banking and other facilities to a large number of users. Costs of providing water, sewerage and power may also decline with the number of users, at least up to a point.

Owing to economies of agglomeration, it may often be cheaper to locate new investments in already established urban centres than to establish new centres. Residents of urban areas may be over-impressed by the migration, congestion and pollution associated with increased economic activity. But from the social point of view these costs may be less than the costs of greater dispersal of industry. As for the costs of migration, these clearly depend on whose point of view one takes. To those already resident in the city the arrival of new migrants may well mean a deterioration in the quality of life, but to the migrants themselves the move to the city may constitute an improvement. A social judgement concerning the desirability of migration must then involve balancing the gains and losses to different people.[26]

Needless to say, uncontrolled expansion of existing urban centres is not a desirable policy because the diseconomies of city size eventually outweigh the economies. In judging whether such a situation is present it is important to consider possibilities of reducing costs by a more rational organization of the city's resources. A more equitable distribution of a city's resources may well ease the overall pressure but may require increases in local taxes and other measures which affect the interests of powerful groups.

E. SOME COMMENTS ON ECONOMIC POLICY IN BOMBAY[27]

To round off this chapter, we consider briefly some employment aspects of economic policy in Bombay. Earlier chapters have analysed the dual labour market in the city and the sharp and distortionary differentials between the earnings of organized and unorganized workers. It follows that the employment policies discussed earlier in this chapter (in section B) have an important part to play in Bombay in increasing output and redistributing incomes. The complications are connected with the lack of physical space for expansion of the city and with the possibility of excessive in-migration from elsewhere in response to job creation.

An important new development which must be considered here is the setting up of C.I.D.C.O. (City and Industrial Development Corporation of Maharashtra) by the Government of Maharashtra. The objective of this state-owned company is to plan the establishment of a Twin City on the mainland to the east of the old island-city to relieve the congestion of space and transit networks. *The New Bombay Draft Development Plan* issued by C.I.D.C.O. considers the planning of the new city in some detail on the basis of reports by various expert committees.[28] A notable recommendation of this Plan is its proposal that industrial employment in Greater Bombay should be frozen at its present level and that only 2,000 new industrial jobs should be permitted in the Trans-Thana area by 1981. This conclusion is not based on an optimal location plan. It is really assumed as being desirable on the ground that dispersal of industry is necessary from a social point of view.[29] Limitations of space and congestion costs may justify the freezing of industrial employment in Greater Bombay. But we are sceptical about the wisdom of restricting job creation so severely in the Thana area. It remains to be demonstrated that a proper cost-benefit analysis, taking economies of agglomeration into account, would lend support to such a policy even with a reasonable bias in favour of dispersal of industry.

As things stand, there is some danger that the Maharashtra Government will find it difficult to arrange adequate regional dispersal of industry, especially taking into account infra-structure requirements in new locations and that, in addition, spontaneous growth in the Thana area will be thwarted. In view of the increase in the city-born labour force which can be expected over the coming decade (even in the absence of migration) this policy could be a recipe for disaster.

A possible worry in this connection is that expansion of organized industry in the Thana area would stimulate 'excessive' migration. There has been practically no worthwhile study on which such a conclusion can be based. Our own work inclines us to the view that fears about the catastrophic migration response to industrial development around Bombay are exaggerated. We would go further and recommend, allowing for the various social costs in employing labour, a moderate labour subsidy in the Thana area of around 15 per cent. The calculations on which this suggestion is based are to be found in the Appendix to this chapter. One of the difficulties with actually handing out labour subsidies to employers is the practical one of how to prevent them making false declarations about additional employment. We suggest that this problem could be solved by the State Government not making cash hand-outs but simply paying the employers' share of workers' Provident Fund and medical insurance contributions. We are even more certain that such labour subsidies would be beneficial in other parts of Maharashtra; since organized/unorganized earnings differentials might be smaller in these regions, labour subsidies larger than 15 per cent might be justified. See the Appendix for the reasoning underlying this statement.) However, more research is required on this subject. Of course, these subsidies would have to be financed by raising extra taxes or rearranging existing taxes but it is not surprising that employment policies cannot be introduced painlessly.

Another notable feature of present-day economic policies in Bombay (and which will continue in the Twin City if the Draft Development Plan is indicative of what is to come) is the absence of any coherent measures to help the unorganized sector in which the city's employment problem is concentrated. Extensions of the organized sector (especially new labour-intensive schemes such as export-processing zones) could ameliorate the problem to some extent. But no significant impact is possible without fairly vigorous policies to ensure parity for unorganized producers in obtaining inputs and markets, and channeling credit and technical assistance towards them. Parts of this sector are highly efficient but hindered by lack of resources. A co-ordinated policy of selective and planned diversion of resources is therefore an urgent requirement. It might again be feared that this policy would be self-defeating because of the migration that it would stimulate. On this matter the following two comments are in order:

(a) The unorganized sector itself is not homogeneous. In particular, there is an important difference between workers in family enterprises and casual labourers. As can be seen from the evidence in Chapter V (especially Table V. 6), family enterprises are largely the preserve of natives—families long established in the city in activities such as fishery. There are differences within the category of 'single workers' as well. Single workers who have been in the city for some time are likely to be craftsmen, carpenters, tailors and so on and less likely to be itinerant hawkers. In other words, parts of the unorganized sector are not in fact easily accessible to newly arrived migrants totally lacking both skill and capital. It is unlikely that resource distribution policies directed toward these activities would elicit much migration.

(b) As for resource distribution measures towards activities employing casual unorganized labour, it may well be that in-migration would prevent any increase in wages. But there may nevertheless be an *output* gain from a planned diversion of resources from the organized to the unorganized sector.

The comments in this section should not be taken to imply that employment policies in Bombay would be successful *in the absence* of supporting policies in rural areas. If rural-urban earnings differentials were to widen significantly, migration patterns may change and migration response to urban employment policies may become much more severe. Our concern has been to combat the excessive pessimism regarding employment policies in Bombay. In the face of the large natural growth in the city-born population which can be expected, inaction in this sphere could be very dangerous. There is little doubt, however, that the formulation of appropriate employment policies in Bombay (and in other urban centres) requires a deeper knowledge of the mechanisms of migration and of the technological characteristics of the unorganized sector than as yet exists.

F. CONCLUDING REMARKS

Our central theme is that economic policy in India has been biased against the productive absorption and mobilization of labour. A symptom of this bias is the growing 'employment problem' characterized not only by visible unemployment and under-employment but also by the sharpening of the dualism of the economy. Productivity and incomes are maintained at a relatively high level in the organized sector by tacit collusion between government, big business and trade unions. At the same time, increasing numbers of people are excluded from these benefits and harboured in unproductive and unremunerative occupations in the unorganized sector. We have shown that this phenomenon is not confined to rural areas; the 'urban bias' which some scholars claim to have detected in Indian economic policy has not prevented the emergence of a substantial and growing urban unorganized sector.

Reversing these trends will need a major revision of economic policy in the direction of employment creation and resource re-distribution. Increased taxation is necessary but not sufficient. Positive steps have to be taken to encourage labour-using techniques, products and activities. Of course, if these steps were pursued in an indiscriminate manner, they would work against the objectives of employment policy. Care must therefore be taken both to avoid output-reducing employment policies (except in extreme circumstances) and also, even among output-increasing employment policies, to avoid those which would reduce the investible and redistributable surplus excessively.

There is no question whatever that the main thrust of employment policy will have to be in rural areas. However, urban employment policies do have a part to play, even if it is a minor one. The policies themselves will have to operate on a broad front. They consist partly of changing the price structure to create the right market incentives. More direct government action is, however, also required to mobilize special job-creation programmes, to encourage the development and dissemination of appropriate technologies, to re-direct savings and re-distribute assets. Many of these changes will be opposed by established interests and their success therefore depends, in the last analysis, on effective political leadership.

THEORETICAL APPENDIX

The Social Opportunity Cost of Labour

This appendix[30] attempts to give some precision to the arguments in the text concerning the social opportunity cost of labour in the presence of tax constraints, taking into account social preferences for inter- and intra-temporal income distribution. As is usual in theoretical discussions, precision can only be bought at the cost of simplifying assumptions. Some of these assumptions could be dropped but only by introducing unenlightening complications.

Consider an economy producing a single product x, divided into an organized and an unorganized sector. (We collapse the rural and the urban unorganized sectors into one and assume that migration equilibrates earnings between the two at the margin). In the unorganized sector production requires labour alone; the marginal (and average) product of labour, m, is constant and is wholly consumed. In the organized sector, there is a politically determined minimum wage w. Suppose that $w = Dm$, $D > 1$. Production takes place using both labour and capital; the production function is well-behaved in the usual neo-classical manner. This sector is under State control. Wages are wholly consumed and the entire surplus of output over wages is used either for investment or for re-distribution to the individuals in the unorganized sector who, as assumed above, are poorer than organized workers. Suppose all individuals have identical isoelastic utility functions, $u(c) = -c^{-b}, b > o$; c is consumption and $-b$ the elasticity of utility with respect to consumption. (The elasticity of marginal utility is $-(b+1)$, as can be easily checked.) Assume that the maximand, social utility, is simply the sum of individual utilities. The problem is to determine optimal employment in the organized sector and the associated shadow wage.

Suppose that employment in the organized sector E has already been expanded to the point where $\partial x / \partial E = w$. (This is obviously worth doing since consumption of organized workers and the total surplus both increase up to this point.) Should employment be expanded further? Consider employing an extra man. The change in consumption that this induces equals $(Dm - m)$ and the social value of this change equals $u(Dm) - u(m)$. The change in surplus equals the change in output *minus* the change in consumption.

$$\left(\frac{\partial x}{\partial E} - m\right) - (Dm - m) = \left(\frac{\partial x}{\partial E} - Dm.\right)$$

The social value of this change is

$$\left(\frac{\partial x}{\partial E} - Dm\right) v$$

where v is the social value of a unit of surplus.

If the surplus were to be used by the government for redistribution, it could be spread thinly over a large number of poor people in the unorganized sector making each of them slightly better off. The social value of a unit of surplus would then be $u'(m)$. However, the surplus could also be used for investment. We assume here, not unreasonably, that the government is indifferent between investment and redistribution to the unorganized poor, i.e. that $v = u'(m)$. (Of course, the government might think that investment is more valuable than that. In that case, we would write $v = hu'(m)$, $h \geqslant 1$. The difference made to the formulae derived below would be obvious and the bias would be in the direction of increasing the shadow wage if $h > 1$. Note that endogenous determination of v would require an explicit inter-temporal analysis.)

For organized employment to be optimized we must clearly expand it till the social value of the change in consumption and in the surplus sum to zero. In other words, the optimum condition is

$$u(Dm) - u(m) + \left(\frac{\partial x}{\partial E} - Dm\right) u'(m) = 0$$

The shadow wage, w^*, is none other than the value of $\partial x/\partial E$ when the above condition is fulfilled. Substituting for $u(Dm)$, $u(m)$ and $u'(m)$ from the utility function and solving for $\partial x/\partial E$ we have,

$$w^* = \frac{\partial x}{\partial E} = Dm - \frac{m}{b}\left(1 - D^{-b}\right) \qquad (1)[31]$$

Manipulating equation (1) it can readily be shown that

$$(i) \quad \frac{\partial w^*}{\partial D} > 0.$$

This provides the theoretical underpinning for the statement in the text that the argument against employment creation is stronger, the bigger is the organized/unorganized differential. It also follows, *ceteris paribus*, that employment creation in say special public works programmes where wages are lower than organized sector wages (though possibly higher than unorganized sector wages) is to be preferred to employment creation in the organized sector. The *ceteris paribus* clause obviously refers to the production possibilities being identical in the two activities. If they are not, explicit evaluation of the alternatives is required.[32]

$$(ii) \quad \frac{\partial w^*}{\partial b} > 0.$$

To put it in other words, given the wage-differential, the shadow wage is higher (and optimal organized employment lower), the higher is the preference for equality which is denoted by b. (Some readers might be worried by the apparent paradox that while a higher b increases the shadow wage on this count, it might be expected to lower it on another count by reducing value of investment. There is clearly another margin here for optimization; this can only be clarified in an inter-temporal model in which h and b would not be independent.)

(iii) Suppose $k = w^*/w = w^*/Dm$. It is easy to check that

$$\frac{\partial k}{\partial D} \gtreqqless 0 \text{ according as } D \gtreqqless \left(1+b\right)^{\frac{1}{b}}$$

In other words, k and the implicit labour subsidy $(1-k)$ vary with the wage-differential. As D rises above $D^* = (1+b)^{\frac{1}{b}}$, k increases and the implicit labour subsidy falls. For example, if $b=1$, then $D^*=2$. As D increases above 2, $(1-k)$ falls. This leads to the eminently sensible proposition that in a decentralized economy, there should be a variable labour subsidy within the organized sector, enterprises paying higher wages receiving, beyond a point, *lower* rates of labour subsidy.

We now turn to applying these results to Bombay. This requires caution because of the assumptions involved. Nevertheless the conclusions are suggestive. Using equation(1)we can calculate $k = w^*/w$ for different values of D and b. The results are given below:

Values of k

b \ D	1.5	2	3	4
0.001	0.73	0.654	0.634	0.654
1	0.78	0.75	0.778	0.812
2	0.815	0.813	0.852	0.883

Our information from Chapter IV suggests that the organized-unorganized earnings differential, D, in Bombay is approximately 3. If one takes the view that rural earnings at the margin are even lower, which is not incompatible with data in Chapter V, then D could be put as high as 4. Taking b to be approximately equal to 1, as giving a reasonably equalitarian bias, we have k in the region of 0.8, implying a labour subsidy of around 20 per cent. We have also shown above that there is a case for a variable labour subsidy within the organized sector but that is probably a counsel of perfection.

Note that in the model above, we have made the following two assumptions among others: (i) that the average income of labour and the marginal product of labour are equal in the unorganized sector. The effect of relaxing this assumption would be to *reduce* the value of the shadow wage slightly for plausible values of the parameters; (ii) that wages in the organized sector are wholly consumed and the surplus wholly invested. If we assume that wages are partly saved and the surplus partly consumed (say, capitalist consumption if the organized sector is privately owned), this would naturally have affected the shadow-wage formula. However, for reasonable values of the parameters the value of the shadow wage is not affected significantly.

Taking account of these considerations and also the opposing consideration that investment might be held to be somewhat more valuable than we have assumed ($h>1$), we incline to the view that a labour subsidy of 20 per cent in the organized sector around Bombay would be justified. Naturally, many other issues are involved in calculating the shadow wage. An important one is the possibility of migration response to organized sector job creation. We favour the view that migration equilibrates urban unorganized and rural earnings at the margin with organized sector employment being, in general, irrelevant to a potential migrant. We have found no evidence to support the catastrophic migration models. However, we can investigate the effect of migration on the shadow wage, making further drastic simplifications.

Observe that equation (1) can be rewritten as

$$w^* = Dm - \left(\frac{Dm - m}{s} \right)$$

where

$$s = \frac{b(D-1)}{1 - D^{-b}}$$

Evidently, s is the utility price of a unit of surplus in relation to the increased consumption. We now keep s constant to simplify the analysis. If the migration response to an extra organized job is z then on the simplest assumptions

$$w^* = Dm - \left(\frac{Dm - zm}{s}\right) \qquad (2)$$

in the case where no distinction is made between the rural and urban unorganized sectors.

Clearly, the magnitude of z has a very important influence on w^*. Consider the simplest 'catastrophic' migration model discussed in the body of the chapter. In that model, migration is governed by the condition $m = pw$, where p is the probability of getting an organized sector job. With m and w constant, p is also fixed. In the simplest version of the model p is equal to employment divided by the labour force. Then, as shown in the chapter,

$$z = \frac{1}{p} = \frac{w}{m}.$$

Substitution of $z = w/m$ in equation (2) above confirms the result that with a 'catastrophic' migration response, $w^* = w$. While we do not believe that migration in Bombay is catastrophic, we would not wish to insist that $z \leqslant 1$. Take for illustration a moderate migration response so that $z = 1.5$. Then with $D = 3$, $b = 1$ and $s = \dfrac{b(D-1)}{1 - D^{-b}} = 3$, we have $k = \dfrac{w^*}{Dm} = 1 - \dfrac{1}{s}\left(1 - \dfrac{z}{D}\right) = 0.83$ with the implicit labour subsidy, $(1-k) = 17\%$.

We have also considered in the body of the chapter a model in which the urban unorganized sector is distinguished from the rural sector and membership of the former does not impede job search in the organized sector. But it leads to the result that urban unorganized earnings are lower than rural earnings which is contrary to the facts as far as Bombay is concerned. Even if the model did hold, it can easily be seen that $w^* = w$ only if migration response z is as large as $1/p$. Even if urban unorganized earnings were slightly lower than rural earnings, this would dictate a very low value for p, given plausible values for w and m in Bombay, and hence a very high z which is totally implausible. If $z < 1/p$ we again have $w^* < w$.

The analysis of shadow wages in the organized sector can be made much more complicated.[33] We have not made it so because the quality of the data does not justify this. Using plausibly guessed values and more complicated models we do not find that the results are materially altered. It does not follow from this that we are in favour of labour subsidies in Greater Bombay itself. It is perfectly reasonable to argue that there would be diseconomies in the provision of public services which would be needed and that these should be allowed for in the shadow wage. It is also obvious that there are spatial limits and congestion costs involved. However, there is, in our opinion, a presumption in favour of a moderate labour subsidy of around 15 per cent in the Thana area. No doubt, regional location policy is also an important consideration here but we have reason to think that the proposal to freeze industrial jobs in this area to a maximum of 2000 by 1981, made by C.I.D.C.O.'s Draft Development Plan, is not based on a proper evaluation of costs and benefits. We are even more sure that a labour subsidy of this magnitude would be suitable in other industrial-urban centres of Maharashtra. In the text we have suggested a practical way of giving labour subsidies. Obviously subsidies have to be financed; this involves either extra taxation or re-arrangement of existing taxes.

NOTES

1 We must emphasize that the faster growth of the unorganized component of the labour force is not *necessarily* to be deplored. It is an unhealthy symptom only in the particular context in which it has occurred, this context being the higher labour productivity and incomes in the organized sector resulting from its privileged access to inputs and technology.

2 For a trenchant analysis of Indian economic policy see J. N. Bhagwati, *India in the International Economy: A Policy Framework for a Progressive Society* (Lal Bahadur Shastri Memorial Lecture, 1973). The importance of redistribution has been recognized in the Draft Fifth Plan. However, the calculations underlying the Draft Plan appear to reach the surprising conclusion that the required composition of output is invariant with respect to reductions in inequality. For a devastating critique of the methodology of the Draft Fifth Plan and of the above conclusion see S. D. Tendulkar, 'Planning for Growth, Redistribution and Self-Reliance in the Fifth Five Year Plan', *Economic and Political Weekly*, January 1974.

3 Information which is available for the public sector reveals that the degree of under-utilization of capacity was 60 per cent in 1970-71, 59 per cent in 1971-2, 67 per cent in 1972-3. See *Report of the Committee on Unemployment* (Ministry of Labour and Rehabilitation, Govt. of India, May 1973).

4 See J. N. Bhagwati, op. cit.

5 For a stimulating discussion along these lines, advocating both 'appropriate' techniques and products, see F. Stewart, 'Technology and Employment in LDCs', *World Development*, March 1974.

6 See Angus Hone, 'The employment potential of appropriate technologies and export-based industrialization in South Asia: Analysis and Policies' (mimeo., Oxford 1974). Hone's figures for India show that the production of *bidis* provides 100,000—150,000 jobs against the 12,000 employed in the modern cigarette industry, using imported leaf. Soap employs at least 50,000 in cottage industries, only 5,000 in the modern sector which is heavily capital and import-using. The modern match industry employs only 20,000 workers and supplies 50 per cent of the Indian market; the small-scale and cottage industry sector employs 200,000 workers. One would have thought that suitable manipulation of excise taxes could shift consumption and production towards the labour-using products in all these cases. Hone also shows that the handicrafts sector which has considerable export potential receives derisory subsidies compared to engineering exports whose import content is two or three times higher. Hone has also pointed out the employment and foreign exchange earning potential of export-processing zones. See A. Hone, 'Export Processing Zones: Gains at the Margin', *Economic and Political Weekly*, November 1971.

7 Discussion of such questions is notable by its absence in the *Report of the National Commission on Labour* (Govt. of India, 1969).

8 See B. S. Minhas, 'Rural Poverty, Land Redistribution and Development Strategy: Facts and Policy', *Indian Economic Review*, 1970.

9 Issues discussed later in the chapter will show that such guidelines would

have to be carefully thought out if they are to serve social objectives. For a critique of guidelines used in Indian rural works programmes, see A. K Sen, *Employment Technology and Development* (OUP, 1975).

10   For a superb analysis of these problems, see A.K. Sen, op. cit.

11   The *Report of the Committee on Unemployment,* op. cit., provides evidence which justifies this assertion.

12   The Bombay Municipal Corporation Act, for example, lists 87 trades which cannot be carried on without a licence. The list is very comprehensive indeed.

13   The feeling that the unorganized sector is 'unproductive' has diverse intellectual origins. Marxists might argue that unorganized labour is unproductive in that it does not produce surplus value but instead uses surplus value for purposes other than accumulation. Hence it is irrelevant to economic progress which depends upon accumulation. It might be further argued (with suitable quotations from Marx) that such labour lacks revolutionary potential. This view ignores the fact that the unorganized sector contains not only domestic servants, shoeshiners and so on, but also wage labour and self-employed artisans. The former produce surplus value; the latter do accumulate or have the potential to do so. Moreover, the idea that only the industrial proletariat has revolutionary potential is surely outmoded.

A closely related though logically distinct view is that the unorganized sector produces 'unnecessary' and 'inappropriate' commodities such as domestic services which depend upon the unequal distribution of income. This ignores the fact that it also produces a large number of other goods consumed by the poorer sections of the community. Furthermore, many of the goods produced by the organized sector too are 'inappropriate' in the above sense. Another objection to unorganized activities is that they use *inferior* techniques. This objection is discussed later in the chapter where it is argued that the superiority of 'modern' techniques may be illusory.

The truth of the matter is that the unorganized sector is very complex and deserves to be studied in its own right. Parts of it are undoubtedly very efficient, other parts may be wasteful. A policy of selective help is therefore required.

14   For useful discussions of economic policy towards unorganized producers the reader may consult the I.L.O. Report on Kenya, *Employment, Incomes and Equality* (Geneva, 1972). The motivation of this Report is similar to ours and we have learned much from reading it.

15   Many arithmetical exercises have been conducted by economists to show that there is not enough land to redistribute among the rural population so that the resulting units are economically viable. This does not mean that land reform is useless but that it cannot solve the whole problem of landless labour. Rural works would still be necessary.

16   For discussions of topics relevant to this section, we would recommend in particular, F. Stewart and P. Streeten, 'Conflicts between employment and output objectives', *Oxford Economic Papers* (OUP, 1971); A.K. Sen, op. cit., and I.M.D. Little and J.A. Mirrlees, *Project Appraisal and Planning for Developing Countries* (London 1974).

17 The trade-off between present and future consumption is extensively dis-
    cussed in A.K. Sen, op. cit. and Little and Mirrlees, op. cit.

18 Little and Mirrlees, op. cit., do show awareness of this issue.

19 See C. Rosser, *Urbanization in India* (Ford Foundation, 1973).

20 The model has been set out in this stark form in A.C. Harberger, 'On measu-
    ring the social opportunity cost of labour, *International Labour Review*,
    1971. Pioneering work on this model, though in a more complicated ver-
    sion allowing for changing m and p, was done by J.R. Harris and M.P.
    Todaro, in 'Migration, Unemployment and Development: A Two-Secto r
    Analysis', *American Economic Review* , 1970. The model has been further
    developed in J.E. Stiglitz, 'Alternative Theories of Wage Determination
    and Unemployment in LDCs', *Quarterly Journal of Economics*, 1974.
    Stiglitz shows that the result that the shadow wage equals w does not
    depend on the assumption that the entire workforce is randomly hired
    every day. More plausible job-probability functions, e.g. that p in any period
    equals job vacancies divided by unemployment, would yield the same
    result *in the long run*. (The proviso 'in the long run' is vital. If $p = tE/L - E$
    where t is the turnover rate, it can easily be checked that $dL/dE = t/p + 1$.
    In general, this would destroy the equality between the shadow wage and
    w which depends on dL/dE being equal to $1/p$. Stiglitz's result follows
    from certain relationships between the turnover rate, the expected duration
    of a job for the average worker and the expected duration of unemployment
    for the average worker, which would only hold in the long run.)
    Another important qualification to the result that the shadow wage equals
    w is that it depends on the assumption of marginal product pricing of rural
    labour. Suppose m is now taken to denote the marginal product of labour
    which is *less* than rural earnings at the margin which are equal to the ave-
    rage product of labour denoted by a. Then migration would be governed
    by the condition $w = pa$. Given $a > m$, the rural product lost owing to the
    migration response to an extra job viz. $(L/E)m$ would be *less* than w.   It
    follows that the shadow wage is less than w.

21 Again, we have two equations

$$p = \frac{E}{L} \quad (1)$$

where E is organized employment and L the labour

force, and

$$m = pw + (1-p)n \quad (2)$$

The migration response to an additional organized job is L/E as before. The
product lost is $L/E\ m$ *less* the gain in product in the unorganized sector
$(L/E - 1)n$. But $L/E\ (m) - (L/E - 1)n = w$, as can be verified by multiplying equation (2) by L/E. Hence the shadow wage is w.

   Three comments are in order:

(i) In this model, we have made the simplifying assumption that the downward pressure on n consequent upon the influx of extra labour into the
unorganized sector can be ignored. If this were taken into account the
shadow wage would be less than w though higher than n.

(ii) We have also assumed that there is marginal product pricing of labour
in the rural and the unorganized urban sectors. If labour income in either

of these sectors were equal to its average product which is higher than its marginal product, the shadow wage would again be less than w.

(iii) Note that in this version of the model, we have ignored the possibility of open unemployment. To our knowledge there is as yet no systematic model which incorporates the unorganized sector and open unemployment simultaneously.

22 Incidentally, even if n were in fact slightly lower than m, the equation $m = pw + (1-p)n$ would, given plausible values for w and m, dictate a very low value for p. In that case the migration response to the creation of an extra organized job, $1/p$, would be implausibly high.

23 See S. Anand, 'Rural-Urban Migration in India: an econometric study, (mimeo., Harvard, 1971). This pioneering study is as yet unpublished.

24 This statement cannot be made very confidently because the education-unemployment relationship in Bombay is rather atypical compared to the rest of urban India. See Chapter II.

25 M.FG. Scott has constructed a model-embodying these features and finds that the migration response in Kenya is not severe. See M.FG. Scott, 'Rural-Urban Migration aud the Urban Shadow Wage in Kenya', (mimeo., Nuffield College, Oxford, 1972).

26 For a formal treatment of location theory in developing countries, see J.R. Harris, 'Urban and Industrial Deconcentration in Developing Economies: an analytical framework', *Regional and Urban Economics*, August 1971.

27 An excellent analysis of Bombay's housing, health, public utilities and local finance problems, and suggestions for dealing with them is contained in *Report on Bombay* (International Bank for Reconstruction and Development, Special Projects Department, 1971). This Report would be a good supplement to the present work. It deals with issues which we have left untouched but which are very important in urban planning.

28 See *New Bombay Draft Development Plan* (C.I.D.C.O. Ltd., October 1973).

29 See *Industrial Location Study* done for C.I.D.C.O. by Tata Economic Consultancy Services, May 1973. Though we have criticized one of its basic assumptions, this is in many ways an excellent document.

30 Some of the results in this Appendix were derived with the valuable help of Sudhir Anand. Mrinal Datta-Chaudhuri also gave very useful guidance. The theory outlined here will be further explored in a forthcoming joint paper by Sudhir Anand and Vijay Joshi.

31 It may be objected that this formula has not taken explicit account of the fact that redistribution of the surplus would increase incomes in the unorganized sector above m. This is true. If per capita unorganized sector income (inclusive of redistributed surplus) is denoted by y then the correct formula using an argument analogous to that in the text is

$$w^* = w - (y - m) - \frac{u(w) - u(y)}{u'(y)}$$

If the relative size of the unorganized sector is such that y cannot be increased much above m through redistribution the difference between y and m can be ignored and the formula rewritten as $w^* = w - \dfrac{u(w) - u(m)}{u'(m)}$ which is the same as equation (1) in the text.

32 Another suggestive way of investigating the issue theoretically is to construct a three-sector model with two organized sectors. Suppose wage rates in these are different from one another but higher than the wage rate in the unorganized sector. Suppose that production functions in these two sectors are identical and that capital is immobile between them. It can then be shown that it is socially optimal to employ more people in the organized sector with the lower wage rate. We are indebted to S. Anand for this point. It will be explored further in the forthcoming paper by S. Anand and V. Joshi referred to above.

33 A more detailed calculation of the shadow wage would have to take account of many complications such as workers' savings through provident fund contributions and capitalists' consumption. We have not bothered about these because we have only been concerned with rough orders of magnitude. However, some of the data required to make more detailed calculations are to be found in Ch. IV.

Note also that we have concentrated on what in our view are the more important considerations which bear on the shadow wage within the given institutional set-up and in the urban context. Other considerations would be relevant in other contexts. For a lucid discussion of the various influences on the social opportunity cost of labour, see A. K. Sen, op. cit.

INDEX

absenteeism, 135

age structure, Table II.1, 17, 20, 22, 39

Agreement, 113

agriculture
  employment problems in, 5
  employment creation policies in, 153-5
  resource distribution policies in, 156-7

Africa
  rural-urban migration in, 122, 135, 137

Anand, S., 19 n.5, 166 n.23, 173 n.30

Andhra Pradesh, 51, 138

Award, 113

B.E.S.T., 75-6

barbers, 52, 104

beggars, 25, 52, 56, 57

Bhagwati, J.N., 150 n.2, 152 n.4

Bhattacharya, N., 126

bidis, 53, 92-3, 153 n.6

birth rate,
  see, natural increase in population

black money, 46, 57, 156

Bombay
  boundary changes in, 22 n.7
  cost-of-living in, 127
  economic policy in, 169-71
  geography of, 14, 15
  history of, 14
  population of, 15-24

bonus, 90, 91, 111, 113

Bulsara, J. F., 34 n.14, 103 n.3, 105 n.7, 107, 109, 109 n.11, 125, 128

Calcutta, 14

capacity utilization, 151 n.3, 153

Chatterjee, G. S., 126

C.I.D.C.O., 35, 37, 38, 169, 169 ns.28 & 29, 173

Commissioner of Labour, Bombay, 99, 113

Committee of Experts on Unemployment Estimates, 3 n.2

Committee on Unemployment, 151 n.3, 156 n.11

commuters, 31, 72-3, 75

composition of output and consumption, 152-3

concentration indices, 138-46

construction, 50-1, 56, 92, 97, 138, 140, 151

contact men, 46

contacts and job-fixing, 132-4, 166-7

contract labourers, 47, 50, 51

cost of labour to employer, 101

cost-of-living, 90, 101, 103, 109, 111-12
  rural/urban comparison of, 124-7, 128-9

cotton mills, 14, 19, 62-5, 65 n.9, 67, 94, 98, 100, 111, 135, 138
  see, textiles

credit, 45, 156

cross-section analysis as a substitute for longitudinal surveys, 139-40

Dandekar, V. M., 108 n.9, 128 n.5

Dantwala, M. L., 6 n.5

Datta-Chaudhuri, M., 173 n.30

Dearness Allowance, 90, 98, 108

dependants, 97, 108-10, 129, 131